"Helen and Art Pasanen are fellow Gideons and godly good friends. Helen's thoughts are inspired, touched by God, and strike a spiritual chord in my heart and daily life. I found even more spiritual depth and meaning on subsequent readings. In these last days, read, absorb and grow deeper in God."

Dr. Ralph I. Greene, B.A., B.Ed., M.Ed., Ed.D
Teacher, Lecturer, Professor, Supervisory Officer
Brampton, Ontario, Canada

"When I first met Helen Pasanen some thirteen years ago she gave me a copy of the daily devotional calendar she had written and published. I have read it faithfully everyday since 2005 and certainly do not hesitate to highly recommend it. I look forward to reading the devotional she has just written: it is a great way to start one's day, a real blessing."

Jean Whittle
Haileybury, Ontario, Canada

LISTEN,
God Is Calling

HELEN S. PASANEN

Printed in Canada

ISBN: 978-1-4866-1705-0

Word Alive Press
119 De Baets Street Winnipeg, MB R2J 3R9
www.wordalivepress.ca

MIX
Paper from
responsible sources
FSC® C016245

Cataloguing in Publication information can be obtained from Library and Archives Canada.

ACKNOWLEDGEMENTS

To God be the glory.

My husband, Arthur, always believed the prophetic messages I received should be shared with others. He never hesitated when I told him the hour had come to publish them.

Special thanks to Rev. David Caldwell and Rev. Ric Berry for reviewing the contents from a theological standpoint.

I wish to thank my friend Frances Dauphinee for believing in me and encouraging me to publish the messages.

A huge thanks to my friends who are prayer warriors and who prayed for me. As a result, the FIRE of God's love continues to be renewed in me.

I dedicate this book to my friend Linda Mitchell.

INTRODUCTION

I frequently say, 'I do not know why God's grace has abounded in my life so richly.'

At the age of twenty-five, I had a conversion experience after watching Dr. Billy Graham on television. I asked God to reveal Himself in a very special way. Throughout my life He has done that, and I still treasure His Presence and His Word above all things.

Spiritual experiences continue to this day. A near-death experience gave me a strong sense of mission to tell others that our Heavenly Father is only a prayer away, and that through His Son, Jesus Christ, there is acceptance and salvation.

I was fifty years old when I became an ordained minister, and now hold credentials with Global Christian Ministry Forum in Canada.

In the mid 1980s, God began speaking to me in my prayer times. I wrote down those messages and eventually LISTEN, GOD IS CALLING was birthed.

It is my prayer that these written words will encourage many readers of this calendar to capture the wonder of God's love for themselves. Pray that He will reveal His heart to you as you meditate on each of the brief devotions, each day of the year.

listen

JANUARY

GOD IS CALLING

JANUARY 1

Deadbolts on doors make it more difficult for robbers to enter a home. Some of My people have installed deadbolts that make it difficult for Me to have access to their hearts. They turn the key and lock Me out of their lives as I attempt to speak a word to them. Ask Me to remove the deadbolts you have installed in your mind and spirit. I want you to know that I am not your enemy. I am your Friend.

JANUARY 2

Deep within every human breast is a longing to know Me, their Creator. In search of contentment and peace, people strive in all directions, but they don't come to the cross of redemption. My words of salvation are simple and offer water to a thirsting soul. Seek no further than Me. Receive My free gift of life today. I am knocking at your heart (Revelations 3:20). The latch is on your side. Open the door and welcome Me.

JANUARY 3

I accept a broken and contrite heart (Psalm 51:17). I will put My laws deep within your spirit so that you will know which paths to take. Study My Son, Jesus Christ's example. Desire holiness for I expect it. Begin afresh each day by abiding in My word for without Me you can do nothing of eternal value. Follow after righteousness and truth, for I am the Way, the Truth, and the Life (John 14:6).

JANUARY 4

I am not like a meteorologist who often inaccurately predicts the weather. I am the One who brings the rains, fills the clouds with moisture, and sends the wind in different directions, as I choose. I need you to be flexible to move with My Spirit so I can send you anywhere, at anytime, wherever a need arises. I bought you with My precious blood and I have chosen you.

JANUARY 5

Blessed is the person who knows Me by My names. Get to know the meanings of My names for that is how I want to be known by My people. Searching My Holy Word, the Bible, is how you come to know what kind of God I am and to know all I desire for you. Open your heart to Me in a fuller way as I yearn to share secrets of My Kingdom with you—secrets I share only in the workshop of prayer and worship.

JANUARY 6

I love you with an everlasting love (Jeremiah 31:3). I desire to do so much for you but you put limitations on Me. Earthly pleasures capture your attention. I ask so little and yet it seems so much in your eyes. But you can not exhaust My Spirit's power. I will continue to transform lives. I will joyfully give out of the treasuries of heaven. Will you not trust Me with your life, and draw near to Me through My Word?

JANUARY 7

Be still and know that I am your God (Psalm 46:10). I am enthroned in the praises you heartily sing. I inhabit those praises, and as you worship Me alone, I allow you to sense My Presence. I embrace with My love those who worship Me in spirit and in truth. Do not just sing a song to Me but put your love for Me to work in real worship and see how this experience will revolutionize your spiritual experience.

JANUARY 8

Allow Me to teach you to walk in victory. Lean not on your own understanding (Proverbs 3:5), for I see beyond human ways. As you learn to know My voice, move upon my prompting so I can bless others through you. Call to Me as you would call your friend for I have so much to impart to you. I will direct your path (Proverbs 3:6) and give you strength for any task. Only believe and wait for the saturating of My Spirit within you.

JANUARY 9

Many letters, many songs, many books have been written by people. You are a living epistle written not with human hands but by My hand (2 Corinthians 3:2). You proclaim My loving kindnesses and you know My laws for they are written on your heart. I write the song for your life. I give you the words to glorify Me. Rejoice for the purpose of my living epistles is to bring life to others by My Holy Spirit.

JANUARY 10

Are you stilling yourself before Me, so still that you can hear My voice? It is in the stillness that I speak. Quieten your heart in anticipation of hearing from Me. I regard these moments as precious for you are dear to Me. Allow My deep love to penetrate your very being. Enter My courts with a grateful heart, and let praise flow freely. I will meet with you as you choose to meet with Me.

JANUARY 11

Why is a leash put on a dog? Is it not so the master can hold it in check? Many spouses, children, and other people are held in check by possessive and controlling persons so they are not able to do My will. If you feel as if you are on someone's leash, I can remove it. Ask Me to set you free. Liberty is found in Me, and I would love to be able to release you.

JANUARY 12

There isn't anything I lead you to do that will be too difficult for you for I am your wisdom and strength. Drink from My fountain of living water and be refreshed with bright new ideas. Times of refreshing are at hand for My people. Delight yourself in Me alone and remain loyal to your commitment. I look for willing, humble hearts that I can uphold with My everlasting arms.

JANUARY 13

Arise each morning to welcome My Presence with you. Your silences shall become golden as you welcome My light into your life. I will bring you to a place in Me where you have never been before. You will sit with Me in heavenly realms and you will know My glory. Walk in the light of My Word and realize the wisdom and understanding it imparts to you.

JANUARY 14

Have you walked in another's shoes? I have walked in your shoes. I have felt your pains. When you are in the midst of trouble and suffering it is difficult to sense My love, but I am with you always. I will carry you through the storms and you will come out as pure gold. Without the fire there is no purification. Do not lean on what others say; lean on Me. I am your joy and strength.

JANUARY 15

Are your thoughts focused on Me? Invite My Spirit to come over you. Feel the warmth of My love, My peace. Begin to move by the faith I have given you, for only by faith can you please Me. Love one another. I have made you to be of encouragement to each other. Even your love for each other is My way of comforting you. I have made it possible for you to love each other for I am Love.

JANUARY 16

How happy the birds are to find food in the winter at someone's bird feeder. They sing with thanksgiving as their needs are met, and they are satisfied. Are you as glad to receive food from Me for your soul? Have you rejoiced too that My hand is upon you? The joy I have is yours also. Sing and all heaviness will flee. Rejoice in song again and again, as often as you think of it.

JANUARY 17

I will help you to keep our appointed hour. All other things are secondary for seeking My Kingdom brings pleasures you have never realized before. Temptations will come but they will not be from Me. I will, however, test your love from time to time, but as you keep your appointed hour with Me, you will receive strength and a way out of those temptations. I would that all My people would pray more.

JANUARY 18

How often do you hear idle chatter? Are your words idle chitchat? Do they bring life to the listener? My words are not idle. They are powerful to touch the coldest heart, the backslider who has wandered far from Me. For the dear one who is truly seeking truth will find it in My Word for it is truth (John 17:17). My Word is sharper than any knife yet it is full of grace and hope. Read it daily to extract jewels from it.

JANUARY 19

Practise being in My Presence for I shall speak with you throughout the day and night. As you go from place to place, My Presence goes with you. Do not forget to include Me in your conversations, by so doing, you practise My Presence. It takes discipline but soon you will notice and experience the difference. Trust Me to accomplish this in you, and take note how quickly time passes while we converse.

JANUARY 20

If you were to place a large seashell near to your ear, you would faintly hear the sound of the ocean waves like those that washed over the shell as it sat in the depths of the sea. I am more than a shell. I know and hear all that goes on in your life and I care. As you pick up a seashell to hear the call of the sea, remember to pick up My Word to hear My message for you each day. I long to impart a word to you according to your need. Come and hear.

JANUARY 21

The hour is drawing near when many will worship Me in spirit and in truth (John 4:23-24). I am moving like a mighty wind, sweeping thousands into the Kingdom before I return. Beloved, the hour is short. Testify of Me wherever you go. Do not hold back your love for it will be My love working through you that will reach the lost. Draw your love from Me, the source that never runs dry.

JANUARY 22

Too many of My people feel as small and insignificant as ants. You are not insignificant. You are My jewel. I see your heart and all you do for Me. You have been faithful in the little things and soon I will add more responsibility (Matthew 25:23). I have put My Spirit within you. Come into your full identity in Me. There is fullness of acceptance in Me. Receive this so your joy may be full.

JANUARY 23

I have gifts for all. Stir up and kindle afresh the gifts I have given to you (2 Timothy 1:6), for they are meant to build up My body—My church. Desire to be used in these gifts, and, when the opportunity comes, so will My anointing. Pray for it to come upon you as there is so much to do and so little time before I return. Ask, believe, and receive this new outpouring of My Spirit.

JANUARY 24

Know deep down in your spirit that I love you. I have chosen you to be a vessel, holy and separated unto Me. Be faithful in the little things for it allows My Spirit to be released in fuller measure. I will teach you many things by My Spirit and you will have the opportunity to share them. Do not be dismayed with My people in whom the fruits and gifts are not developed. Instead encourage them.

JANUARY 25

Secure yourself in Me, and you will see My glory. I do not disappoint those who seek Me with their whole hearts. Hold fast to the blessed hope you have in Me, and praise Me every opportunity you get. Your impatience I will deal with. Be still until I direct your moves, for that is when the anointing comes. Wait, watch, and pray, earnestly seeking My will in all areas of your life.

JANUARY 26

Learn to walk before you leap for then you are less likely to stumble. It is the same in the spiritual walk I have set out for you. Your steps will be firm and steadfast. A zeal will burn within you to share My gospel, but you must learn to move only under My anointing. Expect to hear from Me, and the harvest of righteousness and peace will result. Listen carefully to My still small voice (1 Kings 19:12).

JANUARY 27

Do you hear the rain? The latter-day rains have started. I am pouring out My Spirit on all flesh. Many will prophesy, dream dreams, and see visions (Acts 2:17). Believe I can work through you to reach the dying and the lost. My grace is extended to this generation. My life is available to all who will trust Me and repent of their complacency and dead works. Come to the living water and drink of Me.

JANUARY 28

Richness in My love is found only as you perceive what it cost Me to redeem humankind. I have come that you may enjoy life to the fullest. A branch in My church is worth a great deal. My life flows through all branches alike, giving vitality and sap to all who are joined to Me, the Vine (John 15). As you draw your strength from Me, you will know it is supernatural and divine in nature.

JANUARY 29

I delight to make amends in a relationship. It takes a willing heart to be reconciled to another. Desire a spirit of reconciliation first with Me and then with one another. A restored relationship is precious in My eyes. Angels rejoice when a sinner repents and is reconciled to Me (Luke 15:10) but I rejoice when you forgive and love as I have forgiven and loved you. Make love your aim for it conquers great obstacles in life.

JANUARY 30

The hoarfrost on the trees is My handiwork. I delight to create beauty for you to enjoy. When I created the heavens and the earth and all within them, did I not say, 'It was good' (Genesis 1)? For those who see with spiritual eyes, there is hidden beauty in everything. Look to the good in others and desire only good for all. That is how I see those who have accepted Me – washed clean, spotless, pure before My throne (Ephesians 5:26).

JANUARY 31

There are many dead works in My people's lives. I never intended for My own to burn the candle at both ends and to grow weary. My work and purpose for each of My children is unique, and each must seek My will for their lives. Dead works bring separation. Never underestimate quality time with Me. Eternal dividends are in store for those who ask, seek My fellowship and knock at My door of opportunities.

listen

FEBRUARY

GOD IS CALLING

FEBRUARY 1

Agitation will come into most relationships but be on the lookout, as the enemy Satan would use this to divide and cause disunity. Remember the weapons I have given to you for tearing down strongholds (2 Corinthians 10:3-5); they are not those of the world but mighty. Come often into My Presence as I long to hear of your feelings and hurts. I came to bind up your brokenness and to rescue you from captivity. I am your place of rest, My beloved.

FEBRUARY 2

Can you not sense My Presence more as you have determined to spend time in communion with Me? I long this for all My people. There is nothing like it—nothing can compare with My Presence and My peace. It is inexpressible with mere human words. Why do you allow idols to lure you away from Me? What they have to offer is temporary, and they lead you to believe lies which are direct from hell.

FEBRUARY 3

Just as a kettle filled with water steams as the boiling point is reached, there will be things from deep within you that will boil up so that you cannot contain them. You must release the words I give you for only then will you find release in your spirit. Some people are like steaming kettles: they do best in the heat of controversy and pressure. Labour is not in vain if I am in it.

FEBRUARY 4

Do not forgot that I have spoken through My prophets. Their messages of obedience and submission still stand. Is it so hard to yield your will to Me? My Word encourages you to prove for yourself that My promises are true. You need to do that in order to appreciate My ways. It is all part of growing in trust. A strong trust deepens our relationship and gives you freedom to express your longings and to be yourself with Me.

FEBRUARY 5

Accept Me, and accept My Word for it is truth and life. Know that My Word is a personal word to each of My children. Believe that it is for you, and move in accordance with it. Does not any relationship, even at the human level, involve trust and honesty in communication? Take My Word to heart for what is in your heart determines how you live through your daily circumstances.

FEBRUARY 6

Go on to maturity. This means leaving behind the elementary and accepting the more challenging. Knowing Me and My Word working in you, and giving My Holy Spirit free reign enables you to move toward greater maturity. Put away childish behaviour (1 Corinthians 13:11) for it is based on selfishness. Voice your thoughts upward to Me for I am willing to guide, direct and mould you.

FEBRUARY 7

In My everlasting love there are allowances. You are permitted to do your own will but you will find that you are happy only for a season. Being outside My will brings anxieties, frustrations and dead ends. You have experienced them already. Choose whom you will follow this day (Joshua 24:15). I offer grace, comfort, adventure and love. There is never a dull experience in Me.

FEBRUARY 8

Many shrubs and even trees produce fruit for birds and animals alike. You are bearing fruit you are not even aware of. Seeds you have sown in years past have taken root, and trees of righteousness have sprung up. Do not look at what you consider failures for there is fruit that has resulted from your faithfulness to Me. Keep sowing My Word.

FEBRUARY 9

Speak forth My Word as it is written. Faith will come to the hearer for My Word will not return to Me void (Isaiah 55:11). It accomplishes far beyond all you see or comprehend. I am about to do miracles in your midst. Only believe. Lay hands on the sick, praying in My name, and they shall recover (Mark 16:17-18). I will be glorified in My remnant in this generation. It will be by My Spirit that I shall accomplish signs and wonders.

FEBRUARY 10

Look not to the past for you cannot change it. Fix your eyes on Me. I remove any guilt you may carry from past involvements. My cleansing is thorough and I remember your sins no more (Hebrews 8:12). Each day, come before Me for cleansing of wrong thoughts, motives, and actions, for I am quick to forgive and forget. Forgive yourself, trusting that My forgiveness is reality.

FEBRUARY 11

Do not be deceived by the enemy into thinking that your way is the best and only way. I know the beginning from the end, therefore, I know what is best at all times. My advantage is in My omniscience. The downfall of many leaders happens when they feel secure in their own judgments ,and plow crooked paths for themselves and their countries.

FEBRUARY 12

I created this world for you to enjoy, and I created you to enjoy My fellowship, but many have turned to worship instead the things I have created. I hold this globe called Earth in My hands. I have also engraved you in the palm of My hand (Isaiah 49:16). You are constantly on My heart. Don't stray out of My arena nor My reach, or you too will be tempted by evil-doers.

FEBRUARY 13

Waves are coming. Waves that are created by My Spirit are about to increase. I enjoy sending refreshing waves upon My people. You have already been splashed upon but there are more waves coming. Do not be afraid, but allow them to engulf you and fill you with My joy and laughter. I desire to flood your soul and cleanse and bring changes to your heart.

FEBRUARY 14

Your silence can become an oasis. Watering refreshes flowers and plants and so it is My intention to water your spirit as you separate yourself from worldly cares, and come before Me. Gentle rain soothes and restores and so does My Spirit as it falls on you. As roots absorb moisture so will your spirit absorb new spiritual truths. Let your roots go deep into My love.

FEBRUARY 15

Do you really believe I can change your heart? I require faith on your part. Faith opens the door wide for Me to work unhindered in you. I do not disappoint anyone who comes to Me in faith. As a Father, I long to give good gifts (James 1:17) and to see the joy they bring to you. Taste and see that I am good (Psalm 34:8) and that My mercy endures forever (Psalm 136). I rejoice over you with joy.

FEBRUARY 16

Many people dance to the wrong beats. They look to music to provide their pleasure in life. Beats in music are not all inspired by My Spirit. People create music and lyrics that draw others into darkness rather than to the light that leads to eternal life. Beware of the enemy's beat that lures you to dance contrary to My will. Joy comes from knowing you have touched My heart with true worship and dance.

FEBRUARY 17

I am the One you can fully trust. I have put in you a need to share but it is your choice whom you go to share your heart. There is nothing too hard for Me for I know your comings in and goings out (Psalm 139). I can supply counsel at any time. Much has been given to you so freely give. Follow this spiritual principle for it leads to My abundant life. Ask for Divine appointments—I give freely.

FEBRUARY 18

As you are active in sharing your faith, you will receive understanding of all the good things you have in Me. See if I will not open the floodgates of heaven and pour out My blessings upon you (Malachi 3:10) as you share My gospel. Life pours forth from the words I give to you, and My Word can be applied when you are not certain it is not appropriate as well as when you are comfortable with it.

FEBRUARY 19

Rays of revelation will come to you as you need them. My Word will be opened to you in My light as you ask for new and fresh revelation. This will cause joy in your heart, and you will want to leap in ecstasy. I delight as you come to Me as a little child (Matthew 18:3), eager to learn from Me. I welcome simple childlike faith and anticipation. Wonder not at the lengths to which I give out of the abundance of everything I have.

FEBRUARY 20

Take and eat My body and drink My blood (Matthew 26). Remember Me in this sacred way for it is the highest form of communion with Me. Be a participant in this sacrament and not a spectator. Join yourself often to Me in this fashion to achieve the oneness necessary to experience intimacy. My body was broken and My blood was shed on Calvary for the remission of your sins.

FEBRUARY 21

Your eyes were created to see only certain distances, but binoculars can bring distant objects into clear view. Long for spiritual eyes so you can see greater distances and with greater clarity into My world. Likewise, desire spiritual ears, so My instruction does not fall on deaf ears. Sin blurs your vision and muffles your hearing. Come to Me for cleansing and forgiveness.

FEBRUARY 22

Seek Me early to begin your day the right way. You will know My Presence in a more powerful way if you continue to abide in Me. When you reach out your hand toward Me, I shall take it and lead you onward. Together we shall climb the hills and valleys. You will see the green pastures nourished by My hand and these will cause you to rejoice. You'll be blessed to see more of the principles by which I operate.

FEBRUARY 23

My path is a narrow one but it leads to life (Matthew 7). I cause happenings in your life that you are not even aware of. In the unseen realm I work things out for your good. I share with those who reverence My Holy Name. Do not think lightly of My Word nor of Who I am. You will see My salvation for I am in covenant with you. This new covenant was established by My shed blood on Calvary.

FEBRUARY 24

Have you ever noticed that My Presence can bring an overwhelming 'hush' or quietness? I permeate the atmosphere with a sweet fragrance of peace. But there are other ways and means to know My Presence. In the Scriptures people recognized it as a thunder-like noise (John 12:29) and a reverential fear entered them. In My Presence you may not be able to stand. Soak in it.

FEBRUARY 25

I have called you by name (Isaiah 43:1). I see your faithfulness. As you remain in Me you will soon move in a new sphere. Signs and wonders will accompany those who believe. Faith will spring up to meet the occasion and a transformation will take place as I move in that realm. Be faithful in the little things for I need harvest workers in all professions. Every tribe and nation must be reached (Mark 13:10) before I return.

FEBRUARY 26

As a wolf caged in a pen at the zoo paces back and forth, so you find yourself restless within. But there are lessons yet for you to learn. It is at such times you need to embrace Me and to share what is on your mind. Learn from Me in your workshop of prayer and praise for it is vital that your endless striving to 'do' is broken. I am training you to recognize My voice and to learn My ways.

FEBRUARY 27

I will make channels come open for you. As birds sing with enthusiasm so will you sing in your heart as you reach new spiritual heights in Me. Before receiving their new fall coats, animals must shed their old coats of fur. Likewise, you need to shed pride, jealousy, competitiveness, covetousness, and favouritism. Clothe yourself with humility and holiness (Colossians 3:12). In this, people may see that you have spent time with Me.

FEBRUARY 28

Whether it be along the shoreline of a lake, out in the deep waters, in a crowded city, or on a country lane, be assured that wherever your feet tread, I am your constant companion. Slowly you are learning to tune out all other voices and so you should. My still small voice has a way with your conscience, and it delights Me to know you are responding positively.

FEBRUARY 29

I have considered your ways and weighed your motives. I am calling you forth to pray earnestly. As a battle rages in the unseen world, I seek intercessors to break those strongholds in My name. My Spirit will give you ways in which to pray. You will be amazed as the spirit of intercession comes upon you. Be diligent in the silences for I will instruct you.

listen

MARCH

GOD IS CALLING

MARCH 1

The hour is drawing near when I shall return for My remnant. Are you ready for My returning? Is My Word anchored in your heart? Be thankful. Do not forget the commission I have given (Matthew 28) and the authority you have in My name—the name that is above all names. Tumult will come economically but you are secure for I am your Saviour and Lord. Be strong and courageous (Joshua 1:9). I supply all your needs.

MARCH 2

Many times My Spirit hovers over areas as I seek out those who are faithful to Me. By faith open your mouth and let Me fill it full of words of encouragement for your next-door neighbour, your friend, your relative. Know in your heart that I desire to use you in My work. Desire My spiritual gifts for they will be needed in the last days, especially the gift of prophecy (1 Corinthians 14:1).

MARCH 3

Consider the puffball, that ball-shaped fungus that, when broken open, releases spores in puffs of dust. Many people in My Church are about to be released by My Spirit. They have been maturing, growing in steadfastness and are soon to be broken open so I can release thousands of seeds for reproduction into the Kingdom. Expect to be released.

MARCH 4

No eye has seen the beauty that I, the Lord, have prepared for them who love Me (1 Corinthians 2:9). Lofty mountain grandeur cannot even begin to be compared with the beauty in store for you. Only by My Spirit can the eye behold My beauty. The present beauty found in nature is awesome but wait till you see My handiwork beyond the sunset. Take pleasure in all I allow you to experience.

MARCH 5

Burrs have a way of attaching themselves onto animals and clothing because they have prickly, spiny edges on them. Burrs of different sorts have landed on My people—burrs such as unforgiveness and resentment. With your permission, I will remove these burrs that have attached themselves to you for they mar your inner beauty. Desire freedom from them.

MARCH 6

As the rains descend upon the earth for the purpose of refreshing and revival so the rains of My Spirit will descend upon those who are sincerely desiring more of Me. Do you want to be renewed, transformed into My likeness? I have given you the tools as outlined in My Word. I have given you more than ample faith to believe in miracles. Come, it is beginning to rain.

MARCH 7

I desire that you see My glory. I am in you and you are in Me (John 14:19). This mystery is to be understood by My people and I will reveal the beauty of this unity. Apart from Me a person is spiritually dead. How often have I wooed you, seeking your attention, and been shoved in a far corner of your heart? How long will you pursue other gods?

MARCH 8

What are the purposes of roots? In plants, roots serve as support, drawing water and minerals from the soil, and storing food. Roots are essential. Because your roots go down deep into My love you will withstand all storms. You feel you are tossed about in the wind but firm is your foundation in Me. Recall My promises to you and draw from the soil of My love. Those enrichments will last forever.

MARCH 9

Have you ever extended yourself beyond your normal limits? If you have My Spirit living in you, you have the ability to be productive and creative. Creativity is My specialty. I give new songs to sing to those who will hear Me (Psalm 40:3). I give new melodies, new artistic designs, new words that express My being, My majesty. I also create new creations as I turn lives around to accept Me as Saviour.

MARCH 10

I rejoice in your obedience and willingness to hear from Me. It is not easy when so many voices crowd for space on unparalleled information networks. What is the ratio of time you spend reading My Word to the time you spend scanning the Internet? It is not difficult to be deceived by the god of technology. Which one consumes your time and energy? Beware of the dangers of new-age gods.

MARCH 11

Are you aware that I prepare a table for you in the midst of your enemies (Psalm 23)? Persecution from family and friends will increase for they do not have the same heart towards Me. Many will miss the renewal at hand for they have not investigated the truth for themselves but instead choose the lies of the enemy. Know in your spirit that no matter where your journey takes you, I am always with you.

MARCH 12

At all cost, be one in mind and purpose for there is power in unity. Esteem others of the Way better than yourself (Philippians 2:3), for this is My will. My power is unleashed amongst thankful, caring, loving hearts. At times you will find your spirit willing but your flesh rebelling. Conflict will rage if there is no submitting. Dying to your ambitions and worldly agendas requires My help. Ask for it.

MARCH 13

The enemy prowls around seeking those whom he would devour (1 Peter 5:8). I am protecting you, and I have My ministering angels encamped around those who love Me and who are obedient to Me (Psalm 34:7). Many will come in sheep's clothing disguised as one of Mine. Beware of their schemes and look at their fruits. Know My Word and perceive truth about such people. I will teach you to discern this.

MARCH 14

Don't believe every whim of doctrine for often half-truths are more appealing than the whole truth. Remain close to Me and know what My Word has to say. If you ask for wisdom I shall give it to you (James 1:5). There is no reason to lack it. My Spirit will bring to remembrance the words I taught, and My light will dispel any falsehood or darkened counsel from the devil.

MARCH 15

Whether you are strolling through the woods or walking on a busy city sidewalk, I am watching over you. If only My people would realize there is rest for their souls in My Presence, perhaps they would pause more often to be renewed in Me. The toil and care of this world will always be but My Spirit will not always dwell with humanity. Take minute vacations in Me and reduce the stress load now.

MARCH 16

Come and drink of rejuvenating sap which flows from Me, the Vine, to you, the branch growing out of that life-giving Vine (John 15). You have seen birds get drunk on the berries of mountain ash trees. Be released to drink more of Me and receive My intoxicating joy and laughter. It flows freely from Me. Enjoy the fruit of My vineyard and you will never be the same. The Father's love will engulf you.

MARCH 17

How are you at forgiving? Forgiveness is a must in your walk with Me. I cannot forgive unless you have forgiven. I have said that you are to forgive even seventy times seven (Matthew 18:22). Be on guard for unforgiveness breeds roots of bitterness and then relationships are ruined. Dying to self and accepting another person with their faults is My way. Consider your faults and how much I still love you.

MARCH 18

Many will stand before Me. They will bring their cases before My throne and justify their actions, hoping to persuade Me, but only those who trust Me as their personal Saviour and Lord will enter heaven. Learn through the prophets and apostles what pleases Me. The follies of this earth are of no worth in light of eternity. He who loves Me desires to obey Me. Anyone whom I love, the Father loves.

MARCH 19

Think about the purpose of the sun. Does it not sustain life on earth? It is the source of heat and light energy. Relative to other stars in the universe, it is only average in size and will not last forever. My everlasting Spirit is needed to nourish and sustain your spirit. Quenching or grieving My Spirit by indifference or insensitivity to My Word puts out the fire in you. Bask in the warmth of Me.

MARCH 20

Leaves rustle, while papers and seeds become airborne as the winds escalate. Are you able to trace the source? Can you say, *this* is where it started? The movement of My Spirit is similar. You need not question but simply expect the movement of My Spirit. I know when you need a fresh new breeze to blow over you. As joint heirs together, we can delight in this new wind from heaven. Ask My Spirit to blow over you.

MARCH 21

How many people do you know who are thoroughly enjoying My inheritance? What is missing in their walk of faith? Is there an absence of My Spirit? Do you personally know My Holy Spirit? Are you not tired of chasing earthly rainbows? I promised the Holy Spirit, and after I ascended to heaven, He came to give power to witness and to live victoriously. I baptize with the Holy Spirit. You need that baptism!

MARCH 22

I share the secrets of My promises with those who reverence My Holy Name—Yahweh. I am the fountain of living water to which the thirsty come for the refreshing of God. How intimate can we get if you only commune with Me once a week? Our relationship will only be a matter of acquaintance. Be not afraid of being fanatical for when I walked this earth some considered Me out of My mind too. Fear not.

MARCH 23

The words I spoke and the works I performed were directed by My Father. The Father and I are one; if My Spirit dwells in you, then you are one with Me. You are in the world but you are not of this world (John 17). My sheep know My name and they follow Me (John 10:27-28). There is nothing to fear for I am with you, and My love is beyond human understanding. Will you forsake all so that others may live too?

MARCH 24

As wet snow lightly falls upon the earth in early spring, it soon melts on the ground which is no longer frozen solid. My Spirit gently falls upon you to melt areas of your heart that are cold from bitter experiences. Those who are warm towards My workings will heal from those hurts so that when you come to Me, you can be bold and ask for My aid. Do not wait long as hardened hearts die.

MARCH 25

S omeone took the time to plant the seed, the Word of truth, into your spirit. Someone else continues to pray for you, watering the seed. I am causing the seed to grow and increase (1 Corinthians 3:6). By faith you accepted the gospel of love. You believed that I was and am the Way to the Father, and now you have access to the very holy of holies. Enter into that full inheritance for you are a chosen vessel.

MARCH 26

B eing open and honest before Me is of great value. There will be times when I will correct and rebuke you. When My commands are broken, separation from Me occurs. I am holy and I do not tolerate sin. I know those who praise Me but their hearts are not set on doing My will. Are you ashamed of those things you have done in secret? Then come, confess, repent, and be forgiven!

MARCH 27

A man, woman or child after My own heart will know the fullness of joy, and will enter into My rest and peace. All the knowledge and education this world has to offer cannot give you My peace. I never intended for your workload to increase to the point that your health deteriorates. Human deadlines and outputs come from greed and the love of money. What is robbing your peace and sleep?

MARCH 28

When you least expect it, arrows from the enemy are shot at you. There will be arrows of animosity, gossip, jealousy and anger. People will fly into a rage when their convictions are challenged, or their self-worth is degraded and their needs go unmet. Put on the full armour I offer (Ephesians 6) and resist those arrows. You are a pearl of great price so reactions of others can be deflected with the shield of faith.

MARCH 29

Praise and worship must be your constant companions. In this state of being you have ready access to My throne of grace. I inhabit the praises of My people (Psalm 22:3). Can you imagine thousands of people assembled to worship the living God and the release of power I give to them as they bless Me? So many sing meaningless words. Allow Me to teach you to worship Me in spirit and truth.

MARCH 30

At the name of Jesus, every knee shall bow (Philippians 2:10). There is no name on earth more powerful than My name. Use it often for I have promised those who ask in My name will hear from Me (John 14:13). Talk to Me as a friend even if it be in the silences. I am only a thought away, anxiously waiting your response. Praying without ceasing is a cultivated habit requiring persistent discipline.

MARCH 31

Many walk without going into the valleys where hurting people dwell, nor do they reach for new heights of faith. Complacency is their way. Be on the watch lest complacency takes hold of you. I make all things new. I love variety and when your hand is in Mine, I will take you on fruitful, and occasionally painful journeys all for the purpose of maturing and growing in My love.

listen

APRIL

GOD IS CALLING

APRIL 1

A ladder is an invention used for climbing up or down. In your walk with Me, have you been climbing or are you frozen in one spot? I desire you to rise to new heights in Me—new spiritual experiences—but fear is keeping you from taking the next step. The only acceptable fear is the reverent fear of God (Deuteronomy 6:24). All other fears have no place in a life of faith and love.

APRIL 2

How is it with your soul? Are you receiving My Word into your spirit? Is it going deeper and deeper into the recesses of your heart? Are you storing it there or are you sharing what I have shown and spoken to you? This secret you must learn: share your faith. Love continually gives and gives. This principle is set forth clearly and those who live by it receive a hundred-fold in return.

APRIL 3

It is no coincidence that you live where you do. Pray for those around you, and give of your time to help your neighbour and do it as though you were doing it unto Me. Can you not see those obnoxious ones as I see them? Do not look at their faults but think of their potential when I get hold of them, and My Spirit indwells them. That is how I saw you from the beginning. Hasn't My love changed you? Ask Me for souls.

APRIL 4

This is a new day for you—a day you have never experienced before. Are you filled with expectation about what we can do together? You do not have to feel loneliness, fear or rejection for I am with you. You don't have to be lured away by the way the world thinks for your mind can be renewed through My Word (Romans 12:2). As it is renewed, you will receive daily fresh new revelations.

Lay down your hurts. Lay down your wants. Lay down your pride. Lay down criticism and die to self. In so doing, new life springs up, life that can handle any circumstances. That is life committed to glorify Me and edify My church. Ask Me to deal with those areas where you have not yet surrendered to Me. Meet regularly with other believers, and be a source of comfort and joy to others as you gather in My name.

APRIL 6

You have a greater need to exercise your faith. You have only begun to touch the hem of My garment (Matthew 9:20). I am the resurrection and the life (John 11:25). What is your concept of resurrection? Explore its depths. Death could not hold Me down for life saturated Me. That same law of the Spirit of life is now at work in you. I live in you to accomplish the Father's will. Know My resurrection power and walk in it.

APRIL 7

P eace. I have secured peace for you. So why are you troubled? Come, all who are heavy in your spirit, and I will give you rest (Matthew 11:28). Stay under My umbrella of peace. The wildest storm can be raging but in Me is a haven. Do not worry about your tomorrows for I am Jehovah-jireh, your provider. You walk out from My umbrella when you focus on the negative, the 'ifs', the 'buts' and the 'what ifs' of life. Don't go there.

APRIL 8

T hink of electricity and how it travels through the system provided for it. Does the power available through power lines amaze you? How much more amazing to be tapped into Me, your Creator. I have energy you have never thought of! Power far greater than that of any electrical system is available to you. This resurrection power heals and even raises the dead!

U nderstand Me correctly. Do not become power-hungry. Knowing Me and having the authority you have from Me releases power in you to do even greater works. Do not limit Me from working miracles because of your unbelief or pride. Are you decreasing in importance while I am increasing? You are not a skier competing in a zigzag slalom course. You win the race set before you only because of obedience to My straight path.

APRIL 10

D id not My love lift your spirit? Love picks up the pieces of damaged relationships, learns from the brokenness, and moves on. You have believed in God; believe also in Me (John 14:1). When you are joined to Me by faith, there is at your disposal a love beyond comprehension. It flows from Me to you like a mighty river. What power there is in love! I never intended you to try to grasp it intellectually—you need to experience it.

APRIL 11

The old, the used and the worn-out I can recycle if only you would give Me permission. They become like new again under My care. Just like the potter remoulding a lump of clay, I can refashion you into something beautiful. I will persist until I have accomplished all that I have spoken to you. I am the One who pours out the oil and the wine that refreshes your soul.

APRIL 12

You have believed Me without seeing Me, and you are blessed because of it. Now believe that I am love itself. Trust is only a five-letter word, and yet can you recall in your experience a time when you put your trust in Me for five miracles? Take Me at My word. Let My love enter your bloodstream and let it flow to strengthen, restore, cleanse, rebuild, and empower you. Trust Me for I *am* love.

APRIL 13

Lameness in faith can be cured. Read, believe, and do My Word. Your faith increases as you get into My Word, and, since faith comes by hearing the Word (Romans 10:17), speak it aloud. I will help you for I desire for you to become a warrior in My army. Desire to know and live the full gospel. Do not focus on what has been or what could have been but what can be! The lame walk and leap and run in My Kingdom.

APRIL 14

Many are the voices of this world. Which ones are you listening to? Can you identify Mine in the midst of them? Are the others keeping you in a worldly frame of mind? You can tune out these other voices. Turn off that television, that secular CD. Learn to lose yourself in praises to Me, and you will have amazing realizations. My voice will become like honey to you, sweet and invigorating.

APRIL 15

In the night a dog barks when it hears a noise even from some distance. Its hearing is sharper than yours for a reason. I am refining your hearing so you will hear things you never heard before in the Spirit. You will hear a heart's cry and become sensitive to that person's needs. Be prepared to obey My voice as to how you can minister to that heart crying in the dark.

APRIL 16

As a mother goose forewarns her young of impending danger so I am warning you of dangers of a life separated from Me. Precious are the newborn ducklings to their mother but even more precious are new babes in Christ to Me. Keep yourself in My love and see how you will be changed from glory to glory. Do you recall your first encounter with Me? I want all encounters with Me to enrich your life.

APRIL 17

Abiding in the Vine simply means daily reading, meditating on My Word, seeking My face, communing, listening and doing what I ask. You are called to a daily walk with Me. There will be times of deep communion with Me as well as times of shallowness. Already you are experiencing the difference. Think of anything that may separate us, specific sin that blocks My flow of grace to you.

APRIL 18

Do not minimize the importance of repentance. Through your conscience, My voice can be heard but you have the choice of how you will respond. It is not My wish that anyone be troubled in conscience. What pollutes your conscience? If you keep My standard for conduct, a clear conscience results. If you throw out My Word, you will not have a holy standard to follow.

APRIL 19

I'm looking for a people of integrity. People who are not afraid to admit their sins and shortcomings, and to turn from them. Magnetized iron which has lost its strength is restored by being tied up for a period of time with a correctly oriented, permanent magnet. If you have lost integrity, it is never too late to bind yourself to Me. You have everything to gain when your conscience is clear before Me. Walk in My light.

APRIL 20

O My people, know the sweetness and joy in reconciliation and know that love is what accomplished it. Are you learning how precious being reconciled to Me really is? In the stillness of listening, you are learning to relax and be at peace. Have you noticed something else? Your listening ear has been sharpened to tune into My voice. There are precious memories that will have far-reaching results.

APRIL 21

Many people will be swept into My kingdom in My end-time harvest. My wind is blowing strongly all over the world. Those who have ears to hear can prepare yourselves for what is to come upon humankind. Share My truth and love those you meet along life's journey. There should be a sense of urgency in your spirit. Allow My Spirit free reign for there is so little time before I return.

APRIL 22

By faith, Abraham obeyed Me (Hebrews 11). By faith, mountains are moved. By faith, people are healed. By faith, miracles are wrought. By faith, people enter into a walk with Me. It is to this walk of faith I have called you. By faith, accept My friendship. Have I not already brought moments of joy to you in our devotion time? Are those moments not alive to you? They have brought much joy to Me.

APRIL 23

You live in an instant society. Many expect every prayer to be answered instantly. But My ways are not the ways of the world. While you are waiting, I perform many things you cannot see, so, while patiently waiting for your prayer to be answered, rejoice that I have heard you. Yes, I hear instantly your requests but accept the waiting period and appreciate that some things take time, though not all.

APRIL 24

I have made known to you the reality of living stillness. There is so much to experience in those silences. The heavenly tongue I have given you—your prayer language—will edify you. Through its use your faith will be enlarged. Should you receive interpretation of tongues, many others will be encouraged. My gifts are meant to build up, and to help equip My saints to good works in My Kingdom (1 Corinthians 14:12). Ask Me for your gifts to be shown.

APRIL 25

Have you ever driven in foggy conditions? It is not easy to travel with great assurance through the fog. But, although the fog blocks your view, trust is needed to go on. So many people travel in a fog when they don't have to. Is there life after death? I am the Light (John 8:12) and all things are visible in My light. Consider the fog patches you're dealing with and bring them to Me. Fogs encircle you but you don't have to be afraid.

APRIL 26

Some will doubt My Word. These same people continue to seek Me but never find Me. They think they can stir up eternal life within themselves. My gift of eternal life is free in Jesus Christ. It cannot be earned nor bargained for. It is received by faith. No human works can earn entrance to heaven. What are you basing your salvation on?

APRIL 27

Have you ever experienced a sense of hush at dusk in the country? A quietness settles after a day's work has been done. It is similar in spiritual experiences when all is well with your soul. Oh, that My people would stay in the centre of My will and enjoy the hush of My Presence. It is not a complicated ordeal, is it? Striving and competition all cease in My Presence.

APRIL 28

What's the purpose of a canal? It is a means of transporting from one watershed to another. That's what I often do: I transport people along and through places to accomplish My purposes. I could whisk you like My servant Philip to any part of My earth (Acts 8:39). I give many opportunities to mingle with all tongues, tribes, and nations. Enjoy My transportation systems. They are unique.

APRIL 29

Life consists of many things. Is your life more exciting and full than it was four months ago? There is life in all I have created and yet you need not look far to realize that life is being quenched in people. Potentials are not being reached. Many people are unfulfilled, anxious, and depressed. They never experience My living Word for themselves. Why do you think I mention it so often? My word is life!

APRIL 30

With the invention of the wheel, people have been able to go to the outermost parts of the world. A wheel could be a device for directing the course of a ship, or as tires on a vehicle. A wheel turns or rotates, like the wheels within wheels that Ezekiel saw (Ezekiel 1:16). Where are your wheels taking you? Are your wheels tuned into My frequency for control or are you still captain of your wheels, spinning out?

listen

MAY

GOD IS CALLING

MAY 1

Never tire of hearing Me speak of My Word. It is not just another book. It is holy and powerful. My Word enables people to see themselves as they are. It encourages, admonishes, and rebukes, but it offers hope. Read it prayerfully and diligently, and then apply it. You need not remain in the dark about anything for I am available to you. Treasure My Word and honour it as a prized possession.

MAY 2

Adopt the way of nature: the way of patience. The hustle and bustle of city life is hard on your body. Nervous tension is eased and your mind stops racing as you become aware of the oneness you have in Me. Minute vacations with Me are not only for spiritual value but also provide health for your body. If you take to heart My agenda, your stress level will decline. I am willing to calm the winds around you.

MAY 3

My glory shall be seen in all the earth. My Word speaks of glory but so few understand what is meant by My glory. The pure in heart and those hungry in spirit shall recognize it. My glory will be manifested in ways repugnant to the self-righteous. Take time to read My Word as that is how I choose to reveal My glory. I honour those who diligently seek to understand.

MAY 4

Again, I say to you, 'Deep is My love for you.' So few have grasped how much I long to impart My love. You know how love affects you when it is given and shown by others. Realize that My love is deeper than any human love. I know your innermost longing and I know that it can only be satisfied with My love. What avenues have you pursued to receive My love? I am pouring it out today.

MAY 5

Y ou have to believe I could make your silences into living moments. I whisper ever so gently into a soul a word of knowledge, wisdom, faith or whatever is needed for the moment. I use a yielded person who is available. It is a personal relationship I have with you. My word is applicable today as it was when My friend Abraham walked on earth. I am your friend, too.

MAY 6

H arsh words from My own people have pierced many hearts. Many have allowed the enemy to use them to hurt others and destroy relationships amongst My own. Be quick to repent of your harshness and be quick to forgive a weaker member of My church. Let your love be longsuffering as you travel on your journeys as pilgrims together. This is not your homeland for I have gone to prepare a place for you (John 14:3).

MAY 7

Pumps are used to make a fluid or gas to flow from a source to another place. They help to supply or fill something or somebody with a needed substance. Your heart is a pump that will work a long time if you treat it well. Have you taken good care of yours? I test your heart for I look for ones that are willing to be purified. As your heart is, so you are.

MAY 8

Travel spans the whole world today. There are virtually no places on earth that are impassable to human travel. I will not return until every tongue, tribe, and nation have come under the influence of My gospel. The workers are few. Pray for My missionaries for they often carry heavy loads. Are you willing to be My witness and to share their burdens? Ask Me what role you can play in My Kingdom.

MAY 9

I have heard the cries of My people and have sent them waves of My Spirit to revive them. Fervent prayers have reached My ears from around the world. There is still time to follow Me and to be included in the end-time harvest. Cry out to Me for those who show no interest in spiritual well-being. I always hear the cries of My intercessors for the lost.

MAY 10

In My time, I make all things beautiful. Awake to the beauty I have for you today. Survey life all around you and the beauty of the changing seasons. Do not forget to see the beauty in one another. Observe carefully those who walk in My ways. Rejoice with Me as changes occur that reflect more of My glory, more of My love through their eyes.

MAY 11

Spiritual food from My Word is your diet. Lifegiving agents are released in you as you digest My Word. My Word is not meant to be a once-a-week shot in the arm to spur you on. What would happen to you if you ate physical food only once a week? I prescribe daily doses of nourishment that enrich and sustain you through all kinds of experiences.

MAY 12

My people are playing games—playing at prayer, playing at claiming promises, playing at believing. Consider the games you are playing. Do you truly believe in Me for your salvation or are you hoping you can make it to heaven? Don't deceive yourselves in thinking that because you don't do certain immoral acts your slate is clean before Me. You need My forgiveness to remove the stains of your fantasies.

MAY 13

Can you notice the difference between a congregation praising Me from their hearts and one that is under condemnation? Come to My house having dealt with your sins and break off from any words that have left an accusing imprint on you. Praise releases My Presence, and the atmosphere becomes energized with My power. Praise Me not only in the sanctuary but wherever you work, walk or run.

MAY 14

To those who have received Me, I have given the right to become the children of God (John 1:12). You are Mine by rebirth by the washing away of your sins. Walk as royalty for that is who you are in Me. The riches of My grace, My love, My healing, My kindness, and My possessions are yours. Come to Me as a child asking the Father. Come unwavering, trusting Me alone. O My children, learn what is yours in Me.

MAY 15

Do you understand My Kingdom dynamics? If the Kingdom of God is within you, why do you look for it in church buildings? Anyone who receives Me has a spiritual reality available to them. To accept Me as your king literally means to accept My kingly rule not only in your heart but over everything you do. You cannot operate independently of Me, your Messiah.

MAY 16

Humble yourselves before Me. How do you do that? Humility means you acknowledge that I have a claim on you, that I am the Creator of all things and that you need Me since you are a sinner needing My grace. Only the humble can perceive truths of the Kingdom. Pride often keeps My people from understanding truths. Satan fell from heaven as he rebelled; pride deceived him.

MAY 17

Receive the Kingdom of God as a little child (Mark 10:15). How do you learn to become child-like? Observe children. They are not afraid to ask questions, they listen intently, they cry unashamedly, they dance and they laugh. They trust you at your word. Let Me break off your sophistication, that superficial polish that tarnishes your character. Then you can be child-like. Approach Me without hesitation.

MAY 18

Spread throughout My Word are treasures. Have you ever had a treasure hunt in My Word? Imagine the thrill of finding a lost proverb or a gem that takes on personal meaning. Some of My priests and teachers do not even consider who they are in Me. How can they relate to their flock the authenticity of My Word? Effective teaching and preaching need personal knowledge of Me and experiences in Me.

MAY 19

Submission is not slavery but a joy when love is controlling you. There is no drudgery in submission when it is carried out willingly and out of respect. Love is the key to submission. Husbands should not lord over their wives but love them as I have loved the church. Selfish ambitions distort the real meaning of submission. The pride of life is a stumbling block to many.

MAY 20

I am He who intercedes on your behalf. I already know what you will ask but you need to ask. Your weapon of prayer can be used over and over. To see and hear My people praying is a delight to Me, and it brings Me joy to answer them. Prayerlessness can be a hindrance to receiving. I honour a congregation who will submit and humble themselves before Me and pray: I will enlarge their tents.

MAY 21

There is no room for troubled thoughts in My children. You can either keep your anxieties or exchange them for My peace that surpasses all understanding. Cast all your cares on Me (1 Peter 5:7). My peace is more than serenity. From Me it flows, engulfing every fibre and cell until you sigh, 'I want more.' Peace is part of your inheritance in Me. My name is the Prince of Peace, therefore, ask Me for it.

MAY 22

Look neither to the right nor the left but walk on the path that leads to everlasting life. Broad paths have too many options and lead to many involvements. The enemy will try convincing you that it is all right to leave that narrow path for awhile (Matthew 7). How much harder it is to come back to My way once you have been deceived into thinking the world's way is best. The lust of the eyes will entangle and enslave you.

MAY 23

A distributor in an engine serves as a means to supply electric current in the proper sequence to the spark plugs. But the spark plugs are no good when the distributor cap has collected moisture and cannot fire. But that is how many try to operate in life—without fire! Their caps are dampened with pollutants of sin that prevent the ignition of their lives for My purposes. Ask Me to send the fire of purification to cleanse you.

MAY 24

How tenderly a mother cares for a child recovering from an illness. With even more tenderness and compassion I watch over you. Do you feel the grief I suffer when My children stop loving Me? Can you enter into My kind of suffering today? In the garden of Gethsemane, I asked My disciples, 'Could you not watch with Me one hour?' (Matthew 26:40). Today I am asking, 'Could you not fellowship with Me one hour today?'

MAY 25

How many times have you seen a rainbow in the sky and forgotten it is a reminder of My love – a promise never again to send a worldwide flood (Genesis 9)? The promise is a reminder of My love. Nothing is by chance—not even the sight of a rainbow. The rainbow results from refraction and dispersion of sunlight in drops of rain. I disperse My light on all who will come into the latter-day rains of My Spirit.

MAY 26

History documents that I walked this earth. It records My deeds and My crucifixion yet, for many, My resurrection has no meaning. People will believe what they want, regardless of evidence before them. The new life I give to people is creating history and is a sign to the world of the reality that I am the Way. Records of your birth and death will be kept on file long after you have gone. Will it be said that you loved Me?

MAY 27

Have you ever thought about how a river can change the face of the countryside? Rivers in their upper stages can move great obstacles. In the valleys, fish feed and breed, secure in the river's depths, but as the river approaches the flatland near its mouth it begins to deposit silt, creating new enriched land. My river is here. Is it changing the face of your countryside? Come to the river and be productive.

MAY 28

Can you identify birds by the songs they sing? I have made songs unique. Likewise My children vary in their songs to Me. You are even able to distinguish between their voices. Variety and uniqueness belong to My Kingdom and I love to hear My people join together in praise. If you have been given a song, share it with the world. Give it away as a blessing for others.

MAY 29

Those who walk in darkness shun My light, fearing that their wicked deeds will be exposed (John 3:20). O children, when My light exposes your sin, do not run away in shame. Run to Me who is able to set you free. I forgive all who come with humble hearts. Your countenance will shine when your conscience is clear before Me and others. Walk in newness of life as you walk in My Light.

MAY 30

Is there a vision before you? My people often perish for lack of vision (Proverbs 29:18). Do you live one day at a time or do you have a vision in your mind as to what you could do? Faith and love enlarge your scope of anticipation. There is no reason to get discouraged for lack of vision. Consecrate yourself to Me, and I will give you a heavenly vision with purpose and hope. Read again from My Word: I have plans for you (Jeremiah 29:11).

Fears of all kinds put My people into bondage. Are you struggling with a terrifying thought and find you cannot be set free? It is time you recognized that I have not given you that thought, but instead have given you love, power and a sound mind (2 Timothy 1:7). Who are you allowing to influence you this way? Perfect love casts out fear (1 John 4:18), and I am perfecting that in you. Trust Me to accomplish it in you.

JUNE

GOD IS CALLING

JUNE 1

ach day brings My returning closer. Prepare the way as John the Baptist did. Repentance is required and is the door by which I am reached. Beloved, your task and purpose is not an easy one, but I am with you to help you accomplish it. The words I give you must be spoken although not all will heed them. Some will turn from their ways and be saved. Focus only on accomplishing My will.

JUNE 2

arly in the morning I can be reached, or at noonday or evening. Time as such is no barrier to Me, but you are often confined by time. You say there are not enough hours in the day to accomplish all you want—and yet I say there are sufficient hours in each day to do My will. The things I did not direct are the pressure sources. Allow divine order to plan your day and see the pressures lift off.

JUNE 3

My grace is at work in you. Have you given much thought to My grace? You cannot live your life to My praise without grace. It takes grace to have the Kingdom of God established in you. It takes grace to know that you need Me. Grace is needed to hear My voice, to suffer, to serve, to proclaim My truth, to worship Me and embrace Me. Ask for more of My grace.

JUNE 4

Keys are used to lock and unlock. I have given you the keys of the Kingdom (Matthew 16:19). Keys denote authority. Are you using the authority I have given to you? Many of My people carry the keys I have given but do not know how to use them under My anointing. Others have locked the door to their hearts and have thrown away the key. My keys unlock unsearchable mysteries.

JUNE 5

As you long to hear from a loved one far away in a distant land, I want you to long to hear Me calling your name. I miss the times when you neglect our appointed hour. There is so much I long to impart to you. The inner person is renewed in the daily fellowship I have ordained with you. None of My children should be lonely for I am your constant companion. May your heart burn with zeal for My fellowship.

JUNE 6

I am the omnipotent God. I am the Word that was made flesh (John 1:14). I did walk among you and now by My Spirit live in the believer's heart. I am Jehovah-jireh, your provider. Did I not feed the multitudes with only two fishes and five loaves (Matthew 14)? If I am the same yesterday, today and forever, more then trust Me to give from My riches. What must I do to capture your heart in this matter?

JUNE 7

Have you seen the hard fungus that grows on old tree stumps? Some grow in the form of a hand. Now look at your own hands. What have you been doing with them lately? What is in your heart will come out through your speech or through the work of your hands. Yield not your hands toward your prideful ambitions, thereby becoming instruments of the devil. Trust Me wholeheartedly.

JUNE 8

Have you considered that you are in a race? Since many of My own do not realize it, they miss the mark and never go for gold. Perseverance is needed in My Olympic races. With joy I endured the Cross and despised its shame so I can now intercede on your behalf (Hebrews 12:2). Are you on the right course or are you dwelling in the past? Runners should not look back. Is bitterness of loss entangling you?

JUNE 9

People tend to look at the appearance of someone; I look directly at the heart. Don't be deceived by the beauty of someone. The heart is deceitful above all things (Jeremiah 17:9). Do you know that you can deceive yourself? Weigh all that you hear, especially prophecy, and be sure to test the spirits. Consider your motives as they have a lot to do with being deceived and praying accordingly.

JUNE 10

Keep short accounts of wrongs committed against you, and throw them into the sea of forgetfulness. That is how I forgave you of your sins. I remember them no more after you have confessed and turned from them. No matter how strong the persecution, deflect accusations away from your heart with the armour I have given you (Ephesians 6). My Word, which is like a sword, and the shield of faith are mighty deflectors.

JUNE 11

You need to quieten your spirit again, and tune into the silence. I have drawn you to be still so that you can appreciate and value the times with Me. I lead you beside still waters (Psalm 23). I often drew away from the crowds to spend time with My Father. He is more than a coach between hockey periods. Do not take for granted our special times; they are always for your benefit and strengthening.

JUNE 12

Stand on the seashore the next time you are near an ocean. Look out over the vastness of the water. Meditate on the significance of water and what would happen if you had no water to drink. Water is so vital to life, just as My Spirit is essential to your spiritual life. Ask Me to baptize you in My Spirit so that rivers of living water can flow out of you.

JUNE 13

A veil can conceal, disguise, and even camouflage what is behind it. Are you masking your identity in Me? Are you ashamed of being connected with Me? Such veils can block understanding, crippling you from growing and maturing. When I died on Calvary, the veil of the temple was torn in half, from top to bottom, to open the way into the Presence of God the Father. I am willing to tear away all your veils.

JUNE 14

A re you questioning My voice? Question no longer. I never share anything that is contrary to My written Word. Do not fear being led astray. My Word will confirm what I share in the silences. Therefore, it is of utmost importance to read it daily. If what you hear is prophetic and from me, it is true prophecy and it will come to pass. In these days many will come in My name (Matthew 24:5), but My discernment will reveal the false prophets.

JUNE 15

The streets are full of hurting people, but many have grown cold to the cry of the human heart. At best, My people will give only their money. And yet I ask, 'Can money buy love?' There is no reason for your love for Me to grow cold. Have you chosen others above Me? Do you know how many are friendless among the poor? Go the extra mile to befriend someone.

JUNE 16

Did you know that a bamboo reed is hollow? Yet bamboo is used in making utensils, furniture, and scaffolding because of its strength. Do you suppose you could be likened to a bamboo reed? At times you feel hollow inside, empty, unconvincing. That's a good place to be. My strength is made perfect in your weakness (2 Corinthians 12:9). I am not looking for you to do things in your strength. I am looking for vessels so My Spirit can move within and through them.

JUNE 17

Do you know what it means to be crucified with Me? When you take hold of this principle, you can say, 'It is no longer I who lives but Christ who lives in me' (Galatians 2:20). The striving to be perfect then ceases when you grasp how My Spirit operates. Upon your request, I will begin to work in the areas of your life where you cannot seem to die to self. Release them to Me so you can get free and become powerful.

JUNE 18

Even in a dry and parched land, beauty can be seen. I have created plants that can survive long periods of drought because their roots penetrate deep into the earth. Desert plants blossom and manifest unique beauty. I have chosen you to be like a rare desert plant that blooms in the hot winds of persecution. No one can affect you for your roots find refreshing and nourishment deep in My Spirit.

JUNE 19

O My people, without the shedding of My blood, I could never have said from the Cross, 'It is finished.' I have bought you back from the law and Satan. You are free to be reconciled to God because of My blood. I was the sacrifice the Father accepted. Ponder the depths of your salvation: it is so rich in love and forgiveness. It pleased the Father, and no further sacrifice is needed to save you.

JUNE 20

D o you believe that the full gospel needs to be preached with power and the demonstration of My Spirit? I am seeking a willing, obedient heart. My disciples were endowed with power and you can be too. I poured My anointing upon vessels who had come to know Me personally, and who desired to give up all to follow Me. Do you have priorities that need adjusting in order to follow Me?

JUNE 21

At times you may feel that you are on a swinging bridge and that every step produces a reaction that causes it to swing even more. Do not look at the valley below nor consider the forces at work against you for My hand adjusts the balances. I will take you over 'unwalkable' places. I will increase your faith so that you can overcome all doubts. As you take steps with Me, you will behold My glory.

JUNE 22

How vast and varied are skills in the arts. To each person, I have given talents and abilities. Many have come to realize their gifts. How can you know yours unless you try to sketch that scene or write that text? I speak through the arts. Creative songs and poetry can speak volumes when initiated by My Spirit. Creativity brings blessings and great pleasure to the one who is inspired, and to those who receive it. Ask for the gift of creativity to come forth within you.

JUNE 23

Your conversation should be seasoned with salt (Colossians 4:6)— attracting the one who does not know Me. When you draw life from Me that is exactly how your conversation will be. Those who hear you can taste and see that I am real. Do not worry about what you will say because I will supply the words. Be in awe at what will transpire when the conversations are directed by Me.

JUNE 24

Be on guard against rebellion in your heart. Without realizing it, My people show defiance towards Me, resisting My Word when I have asked them to do something. As a fruit grower prunes a fruit tree to produce more fruit, I too prune to perfect the vessel I have chosen. As a fire purges impurities, so My refiner's fire will cleanse your heart. I discipline those whom I love (Revelations 3:19).

JUNE 25

What is the true meaning of life? It is more than knowing of Me and enjoying the pleasures of this world. When you choose to cultivate a living relationship with Me, I open your eyes of understanding to new realms and adventures. You will know something of the abundance I have for you. But if the spirit of this world controls you, there is no room for Me as your affections are divided.

JUNE 26

Much too long you have teetered on the fence, being worldly one day and spiritual the next. Beloved, I have drawn you out of this world of darkness. Walk no longer according to the flesh; there is no lasting satisfaction in darkness. Life is in the light, and I am the Light of the world (John 8:12). I encourage you to seek My Kingdom and desire that it be established in you. True life enters the heart yielded to Me.

JUNE 27

What happens to plants when I fail to water them? Is it by righteous acts that you are saved or is it through the washing of rebirth and renewal by My Spirit? My rains fall on the just and the unjust alike (Matthew 5:45). Both are watered, but are they both saved? No. Are you becoming a well-watered tree beside a riverbank (Psalm 1:3)? My river never runs dry, making it possible for you to produce fruit all year long.

JUNE 28

Imagine the labour involved in the life of one tree! What is alive comes from a seed, grows, takes in water, makes food, reproduces and dies? People have their own way of looking at trees. Some remember memories of special trees. For some, trees represent money or income. Do you remember My tree? On the hill of Calvary stood the wooden cross on which I died. Do you recall My death with value? Do you recognize the labour involved in the new life secured there?

JUNE 29

Friendship is a marvellous gift from Me. Do you feel good when you are loved? Friendship means walking together with someone you trust. A friend is someone who knows the best of you and the worst. In spite of your faults, a friend loves. You receive comfort and counsel from them. Often the language of friendship does not consist of spoken words. You love because I first loved you (1 John 4:19). My friendship I offer free to you.

JUNE 30

Your eyes represent the miracle of sight. Do you know that you absorb much knowledge through your eyes? To some animals I have given eyes that function independently on each side of the head so that they can watch for dangers on all sides. Your eyes depend on your brain. Have you heard of dreams and visions? One day every eye will see Me returning to earth. Are you ready?

listen

JULY

GOD IS CALLING

JULY 1

I offer My strength in place of your weakness. Exchange your weakness for My strength. Have you understood how that exchange takes place? Rest in Me. It is in the rest that your weakness becomes strength, strength that is renewed like the eagle's (Isaiah 40:31). Enter into that rest which I give and wait for Me. It does not make sense to you now, but the more often you do it, the more you will achieve it.

JULY 2

Often I have said that I will enlarge your heart. Today I choose to soften it. Cold hearts need to be warmed by My love as hearts get hardened through circumstances. Circumstances can work for your good for I am in them, but if you do not hand them over to Me, your heart gets cold. By giving them to Me, you do not smother your joy and you remain soft and pliable in My hand.

JULY 3

Have you heard of a mediation program for business consumer disputes? A businessperson who makes it his practice to agree to mediation demonstrates concern for the customer, and this inspires consumer confidence. The customer is assured that the mediator will have the knowledge of the service under dispute. I am the Mediator of a far better contract. I am your reconciler to the Father.

JULY 4

Have you noticed how many times I have given a thought to you which was the very thought you needed? I love to reveal and encourage you in confirmations. When you are one with Me, absolutely nothing is a coincidence. Your steps are ordered by Me. I am consistent with My delivery. Be open and know My still small voice communicating with you.

JULY 5

Seasons come and seasons go. Kingdoms rise and fall but My Word remains forever. If it remains forever, should you not know the reality of it? Ancient books are the voices of the distant past and of the dead. I am not distant nor am I dead. My words are living and I say again, 'Draw nigh unto Me and I will draw near to you' (James 4:8). Don't rise and fall with the seasons for I am the solid rock you can stand on.

JULY 6

Why are you discouraged in your service to Me? You are wearied in many tasks and have seen only a few results, but your labour is not in vain. Come apart with Me, even it be for half an hour. Let the truth sink deep within your heart that you need My refreshing in your spirit. Hurry not into ventures where I have not directed you for they accumulate stress, unwanted and unnecessary stress.

JULY 7

Look at a stagnant pond, and what do you see? It has become a collection of debris, air-borne pollens, grasses, and twigs. Many people are like a stagnant pond in relation to Me. Pollutants mar their image and you cannot distinguish them from unbelievers. A stagnant pond is powerless to reject the debris cast into it for there is no moving water. Like the angel at the pool of Bethesda (John 5:4), I can stir the waters of life effectively.

JULY 8

Grieving My Holy Spirit is not to be taken lightly. Confession and repentance must be a daily procedure from the heart. I whisper into your conscience, convicting you about shady areas of little sins. Sin is sin—there are no degrees. When you come to Me with a contrite heart, I will wash those sins into oblivion. Feel the freedom in My forgiveness. Forgive those who grieve you!

JULY 9

I have a special work cut out for you alone. Time passes so quickly and work remains undone in My Kingdom. I can change tribulations in an instant so they are working to your benefit. Which perspective do you hold? I do not accept pity-parties over negative circumstances, for I not only uphold you but My angels minister behind the scenes to bring triumph and victory.

JULY 10

What does speed do? Many accidents have occurred because a person accelerated when they should have slowed down. A child learns to walk after taking many steps, and she walks before she runs so that confidence and coordination builds. How can speed-reading My Word affect you? Much within that Word is passed by without thought. You cannot speed-read, hoping to get revelation in an instant! Try My pace.

JULY 11

I t is one thing to partake of My blessings and another to be in the centre of My will. Rush neither here nor there unless you are sure I have called you to do it. The needs you see are many but you cannot meet them all. I have ordained you to be still and to be taught by My Spirit. You are in a school of prayer and ongoing learning of spiritual matters. No textbooks are needed, just the discipline of listening.

JULY 12

A nticipation fills the heart of a child when a present is handed to her. Doesn't the child anticipate something good? Have you been in anticipation when it comes to Me? Every good and perfect gift comes from Me (James 1:17). No father nor mother would give a child asking for a sandwich a stone (Matthew 7:9)! If you know how to give good gifts then how much more good would I give to My children who ask of Me?

JULY 13

My love for you is like a river constantly flowing. My river never freezes over. I have no beginning nor ending for I am the Alpha and the Omega, the bright morning star. All that I have said in My Word, I am. I am the source of all love, and as long as you receive, you are able to give it away. There is no ending to My love and so understand why I ordained it so; love is the greatest thing you can give away.

JULY 14

You have not yet known the power of My Word. I spoke and things were created. I spoke to a fig tree and it withered (Mark 11). There is power in My words. Do not underestimate what I can do when you incorporate My Word into your prayers. I cannot go back on My Word. You received gladly My Word and faith was birthed. There is more from My Spirit for you, so anticipate the best!

JULY 15

I am pavilioned in splendor and I am girded with praise. The universe is My canopy. Did you know there are different levels of praising, different spheres of spiritual ecstasy? Check out the old hymns and see Who is exalted. To each generation I give words to My songwriters and to those who seek a deeper walk with Me and a deeper level of worship. Be showered with My Presence and manifestations.

JULY 16

There is not only power in My Word but power in praise! Praise played an important role in the life of My people through all generations. My courts echo with praise from My people. When you set your heart to sing praises to Me, you catch My attention. In the deserts of your life, praise Me. Couple your daily moments with praise, and see how light your chores are.

JULY 17

Some people's engines are always on but they're actually going nowhere. They waste their fuel idling—listening to the radio, television or a CD. Their lights are on but they are only parking lights that really do not project very far. Beloved, let your light shine for all to see and gear up to My pace so that you travel on My roadways. Remember I am your energy source.

JULY 18

You are enjoying the fruit of the labour of someone else when you munch on an apple you purchased at the market. Take a look at the apple. You can count the seeds in one apple but you can never know how many apples one seed will produce. In My Kingdom's work, you can have the joy of introducing someone to Me but you may never know how much fruit will come through them.

JULY 19

Sometimes in a rear-view mirror of a car you will see awesome sights. It is never boring when you are parked in My Presence: some people come into My Kingdom head-first while others turn their back and come in backwards. Do you know of anyone who has turned their back on Me? These are strays who need to be brought back into the fold. I seek them out through you.

JULY 20

Have you ever seen a person sitting in a parked car with one foot out the door? You might wonder how long it would be before they came out. Some people straddle the fence, undecided about whether to go over or stay put in their spiritual walk with Me. Either you go forward and advance in spiritual growth and maturity, or you go backwards. The latter is a slippery slope.

JULY 21

Wherever there is strife and division it shows that My command to love one another has been broken. What kind of witness is it to the world when you cannot settle differences without becoming angry? Do not let little grievances become mountains. Put on love which binds, unifies and strengthens My church. Without love, you miss the mark for I work in and through love.

JULY 22

I need not tell you how easy it is to fall back into the ways of the world. Seasons play a role in your priorities as the god of sports lures many away from Me. Am I not the lord of all seasons? Who is your first love? If you feel distant from Me, perhaps you need to look at your priorities. Make Me a top priority in your activities. I give to you My utmost, and desire the best for you, always.

JULY 23

Think of the links that make up a chain. Each link is needed so the chain has a purpose. Each one of My people is a link in a long chain, and the strength of the chain is only as good as the weakest link. Many are called into Kingdom living but only a few make an effort to strengthen the weakest member of their chain. If some remain weak then My whole church is impacted.

JULY 24

Beloved, take up your position in Me, and enjoy your inheritance in Me. As you choose to walk close to Me, I will minister to you, empower you, and show you things you never dreamed were possible. Do away with things that weigh you down. It is time for sleeping giants to awaken out of their spiritual slumber. Fasten yourself to Me and weep for the sins of this nation!

JULY 25

My supply is unlimited and you cannot deplete My treasury. There are many theological interpretations of what it means to worship Me in the Spirit and to pray in the Spirit. Do not be satisfied with human interpretation for I will give you an interpretation by My Spirit that will revolutionize your life. Count it a privilege to enter My gates with thanksgiving and My courts with praise. Come deeper in Me.

JULY 26

Pause and meditate on all that you have received from Me. If you cannot take the time to ponder all I have done, how can you be thankful? Is there not one incident in your life that defies explanation, other than that it was a miracle? Are you expecting a miracle? Pray earnestly for those in authority over you, in government and in My church (1 Timothy 2:2). They have responsibility to abide by My rules of the Kingdom.

JULY 27

Yeast, that wonderful fungus that reproduces by budding and is capable of fermenting carbohydrates, affects the whole lump of dough. Sin is likened unto yeast (1 Corinthians 5) for it affects the whole Body of Christ. Too long have My people tolerated sin. Why do you bother praying, knowing very well that you have not confessed and repented of the sin in your life which I revealed to you?

JULY 28

Although you need My anointing, guard your attitude about it because you may become puffed up with pride. You are not the one performing the miracle—I am. Many do not realize they have My gifts and I wait for them to realize it. My shepherds have not taught them in full about My gifts and how they operate. Signs will accompany those who believe, and rich will be the dynamics of My kingdom.

JULY 29

Are you searching for life while denying its spiritual dimension? I have made you with body, soul, and spirit. I confide in those who have reverential fear of Me, and I make known to them My covenant with them. Beware of those who teach self-preservation. You cannot preserve yourself. You cannot add one day to your life (Matthew 6:27). Working out in a gym is good but I am the One who gives life and who takes it away.

JULY 30

I grieve when people merely petition Me. There is much more to prayer than asking. I gave you a model prayer (Matthew 6:9-13) which, when you study, will give you secrets to effective prayer. When you pray, do you really want to know My heart? Two-way communication is vital to building relationship. Your position in Me affects your petitions. As a starting point for prayer, adore your Creator.

JULY 31

Are you familiar with your internal systems? Inside of you is a unique communications network. Nerve fibres are transmitters, relaying to your brain all sorts of information about touch, pain, temperature, etc. Messages are picked up by sensory fibres and muscle receptors in the form of electrical impulses. Messages are analyzed. But the system in your spiritual network is far superior—it's supernatural!

 *listen*

AUGUST

GOD IS CALLING

AUGUST 1

True sponges come from light, fibrous, and absorbent skeletons of a variety of organisms. Their purpose for you is to soak up liquids. I desire that you not be just a skeleton of bones but that you are vibrant with life that soaks up My truths. Become pregnant with My spiritual manna, given so freely from My heart of love, and birthing eternal life for all who believe and receive.

AUGUST 2

Throughout this world many statues stand hard, cold, and lifeless. They depict a historical act or event, or are erected in honour of an individual. They stand to keep memory from fading. Statues or idols have played major roles in the lives of My people. I am not pleased about this for idols often distract, luring you in the opposite direction from that which I would have you go. Ask Me to remove the idols that influence your life.

AUGUST 3

Fear nothing. Fear comes from a lack of trust in Me. Regardless of harsh words and rejection in the past, My love in you will not allow fear to reign. The enemy excels at instilling fear in your mind, but it can be cast out as you bring evil imaginings to My throne of grace. Allow no entrance of fear into your heart for it will begin to root if nothing is done. I speak of love often – it builds trust.

AUGUST 4

Erasing failures comes with great difficulty for some. Consequently, guilt and fear of failure rise up in them. What can you gain by remembering past mishaps? I am the God of grace and forgiveness. I fail not. Remember it was I who said, 'Get into the boat we are going to the other side' (Luke 8:22). I do not abandon you in a storm – together we cross the river and together we stand.

AUGUST 5

You may not always see My hand behind the scenes of your struggles just as you do not see the many people working behind the scenes of a theatre production. People who think they are doing very little for Me will learn how important their small part plays in the spiritual overview. Faithful routines of little things add to the sum of the whole and you will be rewarded in many ways.

AUGUST 6

Let not your faith become shaky for I am not through with you. Hold on to what you have already learned from Me; there is more to come. When you feel bruised, Satan may whisper to you to launch a counter-attack. That is not how I operate. If you defend yourself, you are doing the work of the accuser. Which is it? My glory or your satisfaction of retaliation?

AUGUST 7

Naturally formed rock crystals have beauty wrapped within them. They are high quality, colourless and transparent. A master craftsman breaks away the roughness to give shape to the finished product, grinding and polishing it to bring out its true beauty. I too steadily chisel away the dross of pride, stubbornness and impatience from My own, My precious jewels.

AUGUST 8

It is not a good thing to step backwards into your past. You must walk each new day as if it were your last, for then spiritual matters gain importance. My stamp of approval was placed on you as you received Me. Yesterday is gone and its actions cannot be undone but each new day committed to Me reaps eternal benefits. Every release of power in your life is based on our intimacy.

AUGUST 9

Do you have a bottleneck in your life? I will remove it so that healing will occur and health will flow. Life will flow unrestricted to those areas that have dried up. Do not take your eyes off Me or you will sink as Peter did when he was walking on the water (Matthew 14) and he focused on the waves not on Me. Hold fast to My promise. Your body is the temple of My Holy Spirit (1 Corinthians 6:19) .

AUGUST 10

Do not neglect what you have learned from Me. In the school of prayer, you must experience some things first-hand so that My word can be made real. How else can you rejoice in My faithfulness? How else can you arise and say, 'God answers prayer.' It is I who walks through the valleys to answer your prayers as well as in your mountaintop experiences to demonstrate My power.

AUGUST 11

You have come to a fence, a barrier. You've walked the meadows and flatlands and now a fence stands in front of you. Will you climb over it? Go under it? Or will it prevent you from going farther in your journey. Often I have lifted you over the higher fences. This one, however, requires trust. With faith you can scale the tallest fence because you see the opportunities ahead.

AUGUST 12

Have you ever waded through a swamp? Each step you took was with caution for you were not sure how solid the ground under the water would be. You are still wading through the swamps of life. I am the solid rock and foundation on which you stand. When you are grounded in Me, you soon know in your spirit just how solid My foundation is. There is no sinking sand under Me.

AUGUST 13

Love is the most powerful action in the universe. Have you comprehended My love for you yet? Love went into action when Adam sinned. Love still goes into action when you sin. I am faithful and just, and will forgive you of all your sins and purify you from all unrighteousness (1 John 1:9). Love restores broken relationships. Love will seek out and sacrifice for that rebellious teenager or for a drug addict. Love them.

AUGUST 14

Are you feeling as though you are in dry dock? Ships needing repair are brought into dry dock. After receiving maintenance, the water around the ship is raised until the ship can be floated out again. Has a wave of adversity lifted you onto dry land, preventing you from swimming in My river? Only those who are dry fully appreciate the living water I give. Learning anything in dry dock?

AUGUST 15

Warmth, love, acceptance is experienced when My love finds its way to a human heart. Through My realm of love, you will reach your potential in all areas. Opportunities are numerous. I turn no one away who truly seeks Me. I see you as you are but also what you can become in Me. That is the nature of My love— potential and more potential.

AUGUST 16

My word imparts My being to you. Have you forgotten I reign on high? I know all things. I know all that you are going through. Don't be confused with all you see. Place your confidence in Me. I have not forgotten your kindnesses to others. In every way you are enriched by My Presence in your life. My people need to embrace the fact that I want you all to experience freedom.

AUGUST 17

As you approach a stop sign in your car, you are obligated by law to stop. I am calling you to stop and take inventory of what is coming your way. Is it a carload of negative thinking or a truckload of the sour grapes of criticism or a busload of hurting rebellion? Will you yield and let them pass by or are you going to plow into them and let them influence you? The answer is within you. I've placed it there.

AUGUST 18

The streets are crowded with frustrated, angry, unfulfilled people. They have not searched Me out. They have not experienced My peace, My rest. They blame their circumstances on others, sometimes on Me. They need to take responsibility. You are also your brother's or sister's helper. Your task is to come alongside them and listen to them. Minister grace and mercy to them.

AUGUST 19

Are you still blinded by the enemy into believing there is no power in praise? Deception started back in the Garden of Eden. It is a tool Satan employs to trick you into believing something false and thus ensnaring you. If you will not praise Me, I can have the rocks cry out (Luke 19:40) but you will remain imprisoned and distant from Me. I need your permission to put the search light on your deceptions in order to free you.

AUGUST 20

What is it about being near a pond, a lake, or a seashore? Water has a calming effect on your soul. Do you know how to find rest away from water's influence? Sit down and give Me your total attention in silence. Think of My goodness, My kindness, My love. Think on My truths, My promises, My peace. Is there anything you consider as praiseworthy and of good report?

AUGUST 21

Enter your secret prayer closet (Matthew 6:6) so I can minister to you. Do you know for sure that the Spirit that raised Me from the dead also dwells in you? Let that sink deep into your spirit. We are one. Is there anything that separates us? Shall tribulation, persecution, famine or wars? No! In all things, Beloved, you are more than a conqueror because through Me you have received supreme love (Romans 8).

AUGUST 22

Can you not comprehend the oneness we enjoy? Can you grasp why I came and was born in Bethlehem? Appreciate such love from the Father. As you dwell in My Word and feast on the nuggets of truth, the sense of oneness will come. You know in part the strength in My Word and have seen the power appropriated. I work endlessly through My Word. Allow it to stir your heart as you seek Me in those Scriptures.

AUGUST 23

As a mother hen would gather her chicks under her wing, I would gather My children (Luke 13:34), but too many who profess to be Mine will not seek protection under My wings. Beloved, do not harden your heart as I long to protect you and take you higher in Me. On higher ground together, you can see farther and you will love the paths I will take you on. You will be able to see even through the darkness.

AUGUST 24

Are you studying to be one of My approved workers? Don't be quick to judge a person for it will slow you down. My grace will allow you to walk blamelessly before Me. Hate and abhor sin as much as I do but show mercy and compassion to those who sin. I desire that no one perish (2 Peter 3:9) and rely on My people to fulfill the commission (Matthew 28) I gave. Many are called but few are chosen (Matthew 22:14).

AUGUST 25

I n the days of Ezekiel I sought for a person who would stand in the gap before Me on behalf of Israel (Ezekiel 22:30). I found no one. Is the day fast approaching in your generation when no one will intercede for your nation, where walls of iniquity remain? Are you willing to be the one who links My grace and mercy with the needs of your country? The protective hedge about family and church weakens without prayer.

AUGUST 26

P rayer is your vital breath. There is a hidden fire that smoulders in your heart and that needs to be fanned into full flame. I trod the path of prayer while I was on earth. When you give no speech to your desires who is the loser? I who re-clothe you in your minds will surely lend My ears to your needs. With joy I give you My best. Labour for food that endures to everlasting life (John 6:27) and be bonded to Me, your supplier.

AUGUST 27

The bald cypress is called that because it is a deciduous tree that loses its leaves to the swamplands where it grows. If it was not for the woody humps around the tree's base that carry oxygen down to its waterlogged roots, the tree would not survive. There are times when you have become waterlogged and you needed a fresh spring breeze to blow over you. Stand in My wind: let Me blow over you.

AUGUST 28

Many of My people are like yapping dogs that complain at the boredom of living. They find it hard to be content and satisfied in the land of plenty. They grumble when they are no longer the focus of attention. My Word says to think on the things that are true, noble, right, pure, lovely, admirable and praiseworthy (Philippians 4:8). Look to those things before you cripple yourself in selfishness.

AUGUST 29

My people are often lonely because they have never cultivated a relationship with Me. Is it My fault that you only devote ten minutes to communicate with Me each day? The proportion of your time that you spend in communing with Me relates to how much of My power can be released through you, but also to what things we can do together. Time on your knees is well spent.

AUGUST 30

Have you ever observed someone caught in quicksand? The more they try to free themselves the more the sand engulfs them. Even the slightest movement of a finger will get the sand granules moving. Observe how you could be in quicksand spiritually speaking. You can never say 'no' when asked to do something. You are lured into needless activity that leaves you buried. Activity is not an answer to fulfilment: I am.

AUGUST 31

To be dead is to be lifeless, lacking feeling, sensitivity or movement. It could mean being devoid of interest, unproductive, without lustre or lacking elasticity. Without a personal encounter with Me, you are dead in your trespasses and sin until I am allowed into your life. Life is unproductive lacking lustre without Me. I stand knocking again at your heart (Revelations 3:20)— ask Me into your heart.

 *listen*

SEPTEMBER

GOD IS CALLING

SEPTEMBER 1

How do you think I speak with you? I can speak through My Word, through others filled with My Spirit, prophetic utterances, dreams, visions and circumstances. Learn to know My voice in all situations, and pray for discernment to distinguish who it is that is communicating with you. My still small voice is often drowned out but My love surrounds you like the sea and my communication will proceed.

SEPTEMBER 2

I am like a shadow in a dry and thirsty land, offering you refreshment away from the heat of the day. The bright rays that blind you are removed, and in My Presence you can see clearly. I move as you move. That should be of comfort to you, knowing you do not stand alone. The nature of My love is to give so do not delay in coming to Me. I am ready to give at any moment.

SEPTEMBER 3

My strong right arm is upon your shoulder. Know the assurance of My love and know that it is I who upholds you. Lean on Me. Do not depend on your own strength for Mine is sufficient. I care greatly about you. I will keep you from stumbling. I heal the hurts of the past. I wipe away your tears and comfort you by My Spirit. Many waters cannot quench My love for you (Song of Solomon 8:7).

SEPTEMBER 4

As a piece of iron is drawn to a magnet when it is moved into the magnetic force field so does My precious Word draw those who have not yet come to Me. Healing flows to their spirits upon receiving My Word. My Word, being more powerful than any magnet, can penetrate to correct any sinful habits of the soul. My Word is a spiritual magnet.

SEPTEMBER 5

The rivers and waterways I have given for people's use have become polluted. Humankind has polluted and separated itself from Me. In your eagerness to advance you have gone in your own direction, a way that often leads to death. Turn your hearts, My children, to Me that I may give you knowledge, and remove those things that enslave you. When you look to My creation as your god you have missed the mark. I am God.

SEPTEMBER 6

What is that agenda you are bringing to Me? Is it your list of things that you want Me to do and an explanation for how you want Me to do them? Beloved, I am not a God of agendas. I would say: lay down your agendas and come as Mary did to My feet to listen, to ponder the issues that really matter. Should you not be asking Me which matters are important since I know all things and know what is best?

SEPTEMBER 7

I have looked upon you with compassion and I answer prayers to show how I care for you. I promised to manifest My glory, and you have seen the start of greater revelations of it. In My name—the name that is above all names (Philippians 2:9)— you shall pray and see miracles. Continue to seek answers in Me, and stay close as guidance is only a prayer away. I long to rain blessings on you.

SEPTEMBER 8

I will manifest My glory to those who love Me. I have given you all that you need to fight the good fight of faith. I see your desire to glorify Me in all circumstances. As the captain of a ship charts out on a map the route the ship will take so I have charted experiences for your life. Nothing is by chance. I have created you for My pleasure and delight to see you come to maturity.

SEPTEMBER 9

A sparkplug in an engine cylinder ignites the fuel mixtures by means of an electric spark. Do you know you can be a person resembling a sparkplug who gives energy to My endeavours? Wasn't My Holy Spirit the one who ignited your fire for the things of God? That same Holy Spirit lives in the heart of every believer enabling you to be able to do the works I did while on earth—and even greater ones, if you believe.

SEPTEMBER 10

If you occupied yourself with eating the right foods, doing the right exercises, and making the right friends, your body benefits but what have you gained that is of eternal worth? Your heart is established by My grace. My food was to do the will of the Father who sent Me (John 4:34) and to complete His work. I had food on earth that you knew nothing about. Your spirit's hunger should have priority. Feed on My Word.

SEPTEMBER 11

So often the simplest solution is overlooked—'It's too simple. It cannot be correct!' My gospel is incredibly simple, so simple a child can receive it. Yet those who come under its power are transformed from the kingdom of darkness into My Kingdom of light. There is nothing complicated about it. Trust and obey. Come and receive.

SEPTEMBER 12

You can never judge a book by its cover. It is not so much the cover of the book I am interested in as much as its contents. Beauty appeals to human eyes even when it comes to the cover of a book but I desire for each page of your life to have My anointing on it. I look to the heart of the writer and long to be in the heart of those pages in order to impart life to the reader. When you write—whether it is a book or your life—be concerned that I am in your pages.

SEPTEMBER 13

Rich benefits from Me are within your grasp. My river teems with life. If you only walk on its shores, you cannot receive the refreshing the river has for you. It will bring some soothing as most waterways do but you need to jump into My river and enjoy the springs of living water that are associated with Me. Come and receive and learn of Me.

SEPTEMBER 14

When you jump into My river, you will produce ripples. Just as the ripples we call static in electronics don't produce the signals we want, many will judge the ripples created by your action to be undesirable to them. They will try to persuade you to come out of the river or even persecute you. They will not bother to test the waters but believe lies. Pray for them so they too can understand My ways, My heart.

SEPTEMBER 15

I will send you to homes where turmoil reigns. People will see My peace in you for it radiates from a heart in tune with its Creator. Stay devoted to Me no matter the cost and My light will be seen through you. Seek truth in all areas and what comes forth from you will be a life-giving message. Dwell in My truth and My kindness, and they shall flow like a river out of you.

SEPTEMBER 16

The deceiver, Satan, is actively trying to deceive you but your steady communion with Me will shed light on all matters. My truth will be given and will set you free (John 8:32) from the fowler's snare. Do not be afraid of the roar of the devil. You have authority in My name to be victorious. He is defeated because of My victory on the Cross. You have the power and wisdom to demolish his schemes.

SEPTEMBER 17

Beloved, thousands are perishing, believing that their works and goodness will earn them the right to enter heaven. But salvation is by grace and grace alone (Ephesians 2:8). In the final day I will separate the goats from the sheep (Matthew 25) and those who think they have earned entrance I will turn away. I am the Way (John 14:6) and as many as have received Me I have given the right to be called My children (John 1:12). Share this news with someone.

SEPTEMBER 18

No weapon formed against you will prosper. In the heavens battles rage. The final battle is going to be fought soon. Put on the full armour of faith (Ephesians 6). I have raised a banner in your midst and you shall see the wondrous works of My hand. Stand firm in My salvation, truth, and peace, and look to Me as your commander-in-chief. Will you ride with Me now and join My army of heaven?

SEPTEMBER 19

Are you playing the harlot in today's society? Have you lusted over other lovers, famous people, superstar idols? Have you allowed them to pour out their immorality upon you, uncovering your self? You can be clothed most gorgeously and inside be a harlot. I am calling you to repent of lewdness. Naked and blind you may come to receive My forgiveness.

SEPTEMBER 20

Pruning hurts. Often you have not known why I have allowed certain things to take place but remember that I know the beginning and the end of all things. Vines must be pruned in order to bear more Kingdom fruit. Jewels shine only when friction has polished the surfaces. I order the storms that give these Kingdom opportunities. Be thankful for them for I am committed to you to teach you all things right.

SEPTEMBER 21

In the depths of the earth runs veins of water. Arteries branch off here and there to feed other veins. Wells are drilled to tap into these. In the depth of your heart run veins awaiting to be filled with the water I give, water which satisfies. Without My Spirit coming in to make a home in your heart I cannot fill those veins. How can rivers of living water flow from your innermost being if you are not saturated by My Spirit?

SEPTEMBER 22

People will always search for knowledge, hoping to discover something that will give them recognition. Consider the vastness of knowledge available to scientists today. Has the knowledge always been appropriated for the good of humankind? Too much knowledge has made many achievers gods in their own eyes. My knowledge tenderizes the heart, making it possible to believe My infinite wisdom.

SEPTEMBER 23

There is a voice deep down inside of you that is longing to be heard. Other voices have drowned it out. Can you hear its faint cry? It is coming from the recesses of your conscience. Tune into that frequency and listen carefully for that still small voice. If there is static you will miss it. Be still before Me (Psalm 46:10) and know that I am calling you. Come expecting a response from One who loves you.

SEPTEMBER 24

Have you ever tried to squeeze through an opening too narrow for your body? You try this angle and that angle but you just cannot make it. My openings or opportunities are narrow but I guarantee your destination. In My openings are things like protection and power to remain in the centre of My will. My gate is waiting to be opened.

❧ SEPTEMBER 25 ❧

Rainbows are created through the refraction of the sun's rays by small particles of water in the atmosphere. Each tiny droplet acts as a tiny prism and contributes to an arc of colours that appears in the sky opposite to the sun. Amidst every trial or crisis is a rainbow that is symbolic of My covenant. Have you looked for My rainbows in your situation? I am the One who stands behind each droplet refracting light.

❧ SEPTEMBER 26 ❧

Do you know there are silent signals in empty space? How else do radio waves send sounds around the globe? They travel at high speeds and can be sent because they bounce back from the ionosphere above the earth. The curvature of the earth allows them to bounce back to areas many miles away. If you believe in radio waves, why can't you believe in My signals? I travel faster than sound or light!

SEPTEMBER 27

A t My word, the heavens and the earth were created. At My word I drew into existence all that was good. At times I regretted making people because of the rebellion in their hearts. Still today many do not rejoice in Me as their Creator for foreign gods and even angel-worship dominates them. What stirs up rebellion in you? I consider rebellion as witchcraft and I hate it.

SEPTEMBER 28

I s your mind a battlefield? Spirits have a way of dropping thoughts into your mind. Do not take lightly the influences of those thoughts. Many have embraced them and depression has engulfed them. Bring those bad thoughts that exalt themselves against Me to My throne of grace. Renew your mind by reading My Word. Resist those words and stop meditating on them. There is no condemnation in Me.

SEPTEMBER 29

I am in your midst even though there may be two of you gathered in My name (Matthew 18:20). Learn to become aware of My Presence even when your body is weak and tired. The love I have for you is everlasting. Not one day goes by that you are not on My mind. I see the yokes of slavery around many people. Those yokes are not from Me. I seek warriors who can set My people free of yokes that entangle.

SEPTEMBER 30

The travelling habits of My people need to be questioned. Often speed prevents them from negotiating a curve. Potholes go undetected. Pause a while and reflect on who is controlling your thoughts, your life. Do you have a navigator? Do you take Me on your travels? Who is that person sitting next to you on that plane? Are you listening with spiritual ears so I can instruct the conversation?

OCTOBER

GOD IS CALLING

OCTOBER 1

All creation groans (Romans 8:22) to be set free from the bounds of earthly living. Deep down in every heart there is that truth that Earth is not a permanent residence. Heaven is your homeland. I have prepared a place for you (John 14:3). Death has no sting (1 Corinthians 15: 55) for I conquered it once and for all. Make this life count for Me. I desire to come back for a spotless bride (Ephesians 5:27) who looks forward to Me returning.

OCTOBER 2

In the end times evil people and seducers will deceive people (2 Timothy 3:13) for they themselves are deceived. Through the airwaves, through books, games and friends come seducing spirits. Can you recognize them? Channelling and psychic readings can open doors to wrong spiritual experiences. Your mind will be attracted to these half-truths. Your belief system is not compatible with theirs. Heed not their doctrines.

OCTOBER 3

I knew you, beloved, long before you were born, before you welcomed My Spirit. I know your strengths and all your weaknesses. I know when you lie down and get up. Can you escape from My love? (Psalm 139) Love fashioned you. There is no love apart from Mine. Love surpasses faith and hope. My love desires to communicate. Express your love to Me in true worship and live in My Presence.

OCTOBER 4

As a shepherd I will lead you to still waters (Psalm 23). The lambs, those who are young in the faith, I will hold in My arms. You are always within the distance of My voice. There are false shepherds with My church; they are perverted, unwilling to listen to others, and they are liars. You will know them by their fruit. I will reveal their hearts to you. Pray for My true shepherds to remain faithful, serving Me in truth.

OCTOBER 5

Do you feel you have wasted your life? Perhaps it was through a divorce or an addiction. I can restore the years that have been robbed from you. The lost time you spent searching for other things can be given back. The heartache, the shame that eats away at you I can remove through prayer. I specialize in restoring and you can find something to celebrate in your salvation.

OCTOBER 6

Have you looked honestly at Me? What perspective do you hold of Me? Can you dwell in unity with Me and My family? If you have a wrong perspective on love, you will see how it can fail. My love constantly dawns new beginnings. Interpreting your experiences requires understanding of who you are. What counts as a good life depends on your standard of goodness. Use My standards.

OCTOBER 7

What are the pleasures of power and hatred to you? Don't think that criminals are the worst offenders. If you take pleasure in putting people down, controlling or manipulating them, you are guilty too. Self-assertion and spiritual pride go against My commandment to love. Take advantage of the position I have in you and turn from those sins to receive forgiveness.

OCTOBER 8

Everything that is done in darkness, behind closed doors, will be exposed by My light (Luke 8:17). All will stand before Me to give an account for the deeds they have done. Can you see the importance of a pure heart and clear conscience? Deeds motivated by My Spirit of love will be rewarded. Take pleasure in knowing your name is written in My book and that it is I who judges fairly.

OCTOBER 9

Do you know that the cells of your body can pick up My peace? When I pour out My Spirit, some people feel a current flowing through them or heat or even bolts of lightning. It is your body reacting to the imparting of My Spirit. I wish that all My children could distinguish between the spiritual and the intellectual. It is a reality that manifestations will occur in My Presence.

OCTOBER 10

How I long to take you to loftier heights in Me. As you are raised to a higher level spiritually, you gain much insight and understanding. Your vision enlarges. Things of this life often shadow the vision I have given to you. Walls are erected and the vision is blocked. Do not neglect the gifts I have given to you for the building up of the church (1 Timothy 4:14). Rejoice to climb with Me and you will find that new perspectives emerge on higher ground.

OCTOBER 11

Ice buried in sawdust retains a constant cold temperature so it does not melt. Similarly singing and praying in the Spirit can retain My Presence with you. Seek those things that have eternal value and do not cling to earthly possessions. Sing in the Spirit and pray in the Spirit throughout the day. This is a key you must turn.

OCTOBER 12

Together we can achieve the extraordinary. My apostle Paul expressed that he could do all things through Me because I gave him the strength (Philippians 4:13). Paul recognized that teamwork was needed to accomplish the task at hand. Whether he was in a shipwreck or bound in chains it was teamwork that saw him through. Yielded and still before Me awaiting My instructions and then obeying will get you through.

OCTOBER 13

Some dig ditches for themselves. Strong-willed and confident in themselves, they rely on no one other than themselves and the knowledge they have acquired from others. They fall into ditches they have dug for themselves (Proverbs 26:27) because pride has blinded them. My word is a lamp to your feet and a light to your path (Psalm 119:105). It will keep you from ditches others want you to fall in.

OCTOBER 14

Believe Me when I say that My love expels all earthly fears and worries. You think you are alone, forgetting that I am making your journey more bearable as we walk together. Expect Me to walk with you. Though you do not see Me, believe. I navigate all the way to the doorway of heaven. The view is sensational from My quarters. Come and partake.

OCTOBER 15

Have you wondered why I created fleas? They are wingless, bloodsucking insects that jump. Everything I have created has a purpose. Some people have flea-like characteristics. They attach themselves to others and slowly destroy them, draining their strength. If no one comes to the rescue, they faint. Recognize when someone is draining your energy and pray for them. Let Me deal with them.

OCTOBER 16

Is there a mountain in your life? You can climb every mountain with My help. You never have to fear for My light shines before you. You see differently in My light and obstacles will appear smaller. My light can shine through mountains, exposing what's within like an x-ray. My light travels on unlimited.

OCTOBER 17

D o you ever have conversations with yourself? Do you think about your nature and what it could be like in Me? May I suggest that you speak to yourself in psalms and hymns and spiritual songs (Ephesians 5:19). Make melody in your heart and enter to bathe in My Presence. Through worship I can amplify the still small voice and at the same time change your nature. You have My attention when you worship from your heart.

OCTOBER 18

I have seen your sincere heart. I shall give you a holy fear of Me for I know the longings you have. I see your motives. Stand by those I have given to you to minister to for I have work to accomplish in them. I am the All-Sufficient One, El Shaddai –experience that sufficiency. All counsel and wisdom is at your disposal so go ahead and do what I show you to do!

OCTOBER 19

The days you spend here on earth are few compared to eternity. Learn to number your days so you use your time wisely (Psalm 90:12). Through the years, you have attained knowledge and on occasion you did not ask for wisdom to apply it. Ask for wisdom in all that you do (James 1:5) and as we fellowship together I will impart that which is lacking in you. Covet My Presence for in it is fullness of joy (Psalm 16:11). My promises do not fail.

OCTOBER 20

A sunbeam shining through a window will reflect off tiny particles of dust within the room and reveal their presence. My light exposes things of deeper importance—impurities of the heart. Though numerous are the specks in My people, they are precious to Me. I am willing to remove those specks so that their countenance changes to transparency.

OCTOBER 21

In the secret prayer chamber, I choose to reveal Myself. I have already shared with you that when you seek Me with your whole heart you will find Me (Jeremiah 29:13). My eyes are on the faithful in this land (Psalm 101:6). All that belongs to the Father is Mine (John 16:15) and I make it known to you. When the spirit of prophecy comes upon you in the night, speak it forth. Proclaim what I whisper in your ear wherever I send you.

OCTOBER 22

Gold may have its value but I say there is something more valuable than gold. Gold cannot replace My relationship with you, nor can gold comfort a soul in distress. Gold cannot reach the depths of a heart to soothe the hurts others have inflicted. There is no use for gold in My spiritual Kingdom. Why is it a priority? Set your affections on things above (Colossians 3:2) and be secure in My riches, My love and provision.

OCTOBER 23

I have given gifts to My people to carry on in My powerful name. I welcome you into the league of faith. There is no doubt allowed in My league. You are called to praise, believe, and walk by faith as Abraham did. Your love for Me and My love in you will always find a way. Excuses come from indifference. Let not your love grow cold (Matthew 24:12) for it is needed to give away. If you don't have it you cannot give it away.

OCTOBER 24

How are you doing with those distractions, those disruptions that keep coming toward you? Has your focus turned away from Me? Take them in stride, never forgetting the richness of the fellowship we enjoy. Realize I can master all those inconveniences for you if you ask. Does fretting bring anxiety? Cast them all unto My shoulders (1 Peter 5:7).

OCTOBER 25

Love and grace are desperately needed. You are judged by their presence or absence by those who do not know Me. My love is shed abroad in your heart, so what is blocking it? Do not hesitate to examine or test yourself. When the persecutions come, will you pass the test? Be of one mind in the family of faith and live in peace. Be there for one another, always encouraging, strengthening one another.

OCTOBER 26

It is not My will to see calamity come upon anyone. Neither should you rejoice when the wicked are punished. I am a discerner of your thoughts. A disco ball with many tiny mirrors glued to it is hung from a string, reflecting your image in many angles; so too I see the one who has fallen. I see from his perspective, too. I am ready and will respond to the prayers of the destitute hit with calamity.

OCTOBER 27

To many fishermen, fly-tying is a key part of the art of fishing. They will go to great lengths to make and tie artificial flies to imitate any one of thousands of insects to deceive a fish. These are not the kind of fishermen I am seeking. I will make you fishers of people (Matthew 4:19) but you will not be motivated to deceive people. If you do deceive then My truth is not in you. My truth frees; it does not snare. I love honesty and integrity.

OCTOBER 28

It may seem to you like eternity before I answer some of your prayers. Beloved, I am not confined by the element of time. As you trusted Me more completely, waiting for prayers to be answered becomes no problem. Are you waiting in expectation? Are you using My Word in your prayers? I am faithful to perform My Word. Rely on that Word regardless how hopeless things appear.

OCTOBER 29

I work on a higher plane than that of the flesh and so you must aim for spiritual health. It comes is the form of discipline and obedience. Striving is exhausting and all agendas must be buried. You are on a pilgrimage. I am your guide, ordering your steps. Learn to pray without ceasing (1 Thessalonians 5:17) and press on toward the high calling you have in Me (Philippians 3:14). Persevere at all cost but in that perseverance enjoy relaxing in Me.

OCTOBER 30

Weeping may endure the night but joy comes in the morning (Psalm 30:5). How hard it is for some to trust Me when circumstances seem out of control. Do you know that when you trust Me you release negative emotions? Faith has a certainty and a purpose. Faith will see beyond the problem and look on the vision of the possible in the unknown. Faith never looks at things to go wrong.

OCTOBER 31

For reasons unknown to you, I have withheld some answers to prayer. My timing is perfect. Allow thanksgiving to flood your soul, and expect the answer to come by faith. Don't look to how I will answer for it is best left in My hands. Often unspoken messages reach the ears of those waiting for My answer. I deliver visions on occasion into your spirit whereby you can say, 'It's done. I'll rejoice.'

listen

NOVEMBER

GOD IS CALLING

NOVEMBER 1

Are you recognizing the other voices that give opinions? When you get more familiar with My still small voice (1 Kings 19:12) and My Word, you will distinguish the other voices coming to you through friends and enemies. Those seducing spirits will cause My people to wander from the truth, telling you to do things contrary to My Word. Many fall, and some have learned hard lessons because of a weak relationship with Me.

NOVEMBER 2

Physical death is part of this earthly heritage. You need not be afraid of it for death is the beginning of your eternal walk. A sense of loss will accompany you when a loved one dies. But do not look upon death as being something cruel because you are born from above and are freed from the shell of a human body to fly with Me. When you envision eternity with Me, there is no sting attached to dying.

NOVEMBER 3

I have not created many flightless birds. However, the kiwi bird is one of them. It has a uniqueness about it. She lays the largest egg in proportion to her size of any other bird. Her size is about three kilograms but she can produce an egg about one half of a kilogram. Some of My people are flightless. They do not fly from one city to the next to speak at conferences but their offspring are giants in the faith.

NOVEMBER 4

Are you still looking for answers to life? Are you tired of empty words? This can be a time of vulnerability for the devil to transform himself into an angel of light. Psychics on television programs promise guidance and hope. All are counterfeits. King Saul sought answers from a witch, a medium who angered Me. I give you the answers to life and freedom. My Spirit can become real to you because I only speak truth.

NOVEMBER 5

There is no voice like that of the person you are in love with. You recognize their voice from afar. Your ears have become accustomed and alert to every word spoken by your lover. Are you in love with Me? I long to hear your voice. I long to trust in your words. The requests you have are many. Shouldn't I be given equal time to speak or will you dominate the conversation? Listen for I have much to say.

NOVEMBER 6

Some feel that they have oceans of time left before they have to make up their minds about who I am and why I gave My life for them. By the time you have reached fifty years of age, you will have had ample time to think about salvation. I have knocked on your heart (Revelations 3:20) many times but you did not answer the door. I am the door into the courts of the Almighty. Listen for I am calling.

NOVEMBER 7

There are rhythms in all life structures. You have within you an internal clock that keeps in step with the sun. You have regular cycles of activity, including eating and sleeping. You have variations of pulse rates, cell growth, blood pressure, and body temperatures. You can synchronize with a change in your regular cycle and adapt to either total light or total darkness. Synchronize with Me for eternal rhythms.

NOVEMBER 8

Be an open vessel unto Me. You have learned which keys unlock the door of My heart. Never underestimate the importance of praise and worship. Anything you lack I will supply. Each day the windows of My storehouse are opened for you. Never be in a hurry in your appointed hour with Me. The harvest needs to be gathered in—many are waiting to receive Me. Hear My instructions.

NOVEMBER 9

Scum is that filmy layer of worthless matter that forms on surfaces of water or other liquids. The dross of molten metals is also known as scum. Most scum is discarded as worthless. Are you feeling like scum? Has somebody rejected you and walked out of your life? Beloved, I came to give you life although people cried at My trial, 'Crucify Him.' Come, let Me embrace you. I know how you feel.

NOVEMBER 10

People run from responsibility, they run when fear grips them, they run to alcohol and drugs, they run to horse races to gamble. They keep running and when they reach their destination, they are exhausted. I desire you come out of the rat race of life that holds you in tension. There is a place to run to: My arms of love, My shelter and My haven of rest. Come.

NOVEMBER 11

Did you know that astronomers use radio telescopes to listen to the stars? Radio signals from space are reflected from a massive dish onto an antenna. These are analyzed to chart the universe. I have stationed stars in space. They pulsate and astronomers can tell when a star burns up. I have transmitters through which My gospel pulsates. You are one.

NOVEMBER 12

I see far into the distance. I see things that are out of sight for you, like the human invention of radar. Radar is made possible again by radio waves being bounced off objects with their returning echo being monitored. Today air-traffic controllers see planes approaching on a screen. I do not need radar to know where you are. I am omnipresent. Come so I can show you the route I have mapped out for you.

NOVEMBER 13

What you project to others is connected with what you have taken into your spirit. If My word is reaching your innermost being, it will be reflected in your speech and behaviour. You are chosen and belong to Me that you may declare My praises as I have called you out of darkness into My light (1 Peter 2:9). Have I become your strength, your song, your salvation? If so, you have a treasure to share as you sojourn.

NOVEMBER 14

Is there a time of refreshing needed in your life? There is so much more to experience in your walk with Me. There are things that weigh you down. Carrying your own loads will result in weariness. It becomes harder to hear Me. Wait upon Me and I shall renew your strength. You shall walk and not faint (Isaiah 40:31). Allow those weights to drop off and come to the Giver who makes the loads light.

NOVEMBER 15

What does it mean to yield to Me? If you did a word study on 'yield' you would find that it means to surrender, to give way to pressure or persuasion. It also means to give a way to what is stronger or better. Yielding thus becomes a positive act. It is to your advantage to yield to Me. I desire to remove the pressures, the forces that bog you down. I would that you move freely—come and yield to your Beloved.

NOVEMBER 16

I equip My people for every good work. A willingness to serve Me must be in your heart before equipping takes root. I love a cheerful giver (2 Corinthians 9:7) whether you serve Me through your talents, time, or money. When you give to others as unto Me, I rejoice. It is time to move on to greater things in Me, a deeper and more intimate relationship with Me. Let not your heart be troubled (John 14:1) for I am doing a new thing.

NOVEMBER 17

As a train whistles to warn of its approaching a crossing so I warn My people that I am coming for My bride, holy and undefiled. Holiness I demand. Let honesty prevail before Me and before all people. I detest lying tongues (Proverbs 12:22) that deceive. You can hide nothing from Me. The schemes of the wicked one will come to nothing. Discernment and understanding shall be gained by holy people. Do not live as the world does for you are set apart to be holy. Come receive My forgiveness.

NOVEMBER 18

Faith will be your portion. Faith will rise up when you need it. My hand will be outstretched toward you, supplying your need and accomplishing My purpose. Focus your mind on Me and believe that I will reveal mysteries because I am all-knowing. Ask for understanding and wisdom, and they shall be granted in measure. Walk and abide in My love, and My light will unfold the works of My hand today.

NOVEMBER 19

On bended knee many come to Me. But with heavy hearts and troubled minds they rise from their knees, never having entered into My peace. How long must I wait before you learn the secret of abiding and resting in Me? I give but you are not receiving. Your praise should flow to Me continuously even in the midst of trouble. I will hear your praises and impart blessings in exchange for your heartaches.

NOVEMBER 20

Would you be able to hear a cricket amidst the noise of a busy city street? To hear would take some fine-tuning. One person might be able but a person accustomed to truck horns and loud music would miss the call of the cricket. The person who listens to Me will get to know My Kingdom principles and know how to apply them. If you desire to hear My still small voice above the traffic, be still often and listen.

NOVEMBER 21

How thoughtful are your friends? Suppose you planned a catered dinner for forty guests. If only twenty guests showed up, you would be paying for empty seats. I am inviting you to the marriage feast of the Lamb. My invitation carries with it a RSVP. Would you be thoughtful enough to let Me know if you wish to dine with Me in heaven?

NOVEMBER 22

What is the distance between you and Me? You can reach for a phone and call a friend thousands of miles away, but to reach Me immediately, you do not have to dial a phone. No communication lines, no satellite receptors, nothing compares to the communication system I have available by My Spirit. I know your thoughts from far off and the struggle you have aligning them with Mine. Toll free, call Me.

NOVEMBER 23

Without thinking about it, you brace yourself when you begin to fall. You do this automatically to help prevent serious injury. People will cushion their physical falls but when it comes to spiritual falls, they don't think much about preventing them. Shouldn't cushioning a spiritual fall be important? Signs, symptoms are evident—love cools, talk stops. Return to Me.

NOVEMBER 24

Being caught up with the god of materialism prevents you from accepting and using My gifts. How I desire to see My gifts operational in My church. Unbelief reigns because you don't have a clue what I have done for you nor what I offer every day! You will accept gifts from friends so why do you hesitate to receive Mine? Why are you so afraid to step out in faith and receive from Me?

NOVEMBER 25

Tough times are in store for many around the world. I grieve. The present economic system is rocky. Do you know the secrets of living in tough times? What should be your concentration? Will you be able to live on bare necessities and help others out too? Your faithfulness to Me and others counts as righteousness. I will multiply the loaves and the fishes (John 6) in tough times.

NOVEMBER 26

Guilt resembles a rodent's behaviour. Rats and beavers have large incisor teeth which never stop growing. They are used for gnawing. To gnaw means to cause constant distress. This is the pattern guilt takes in you. What is gnawing at your conscience? Confession is good for the soul. Repentance too is needed. No sin surprises Me. Come, confess, repent—your gnawing will be silenced. I forgive.

NOVEMBER 27

Come to Me as a child would come to a parent to receive acceptance and love. The nature of My love assures and comforts. In My Presence, anxieties melt, and hope springs up for better tomorrows. Enter into My sanctuary to experience wholeness and relaxation. The hour of power in prayer gives much courage to face each new day. Do not let the tempter convince you otherwise.

NOVEMBER 28

Have you seen a solar or lunar eclipse? That's when the earth and moon cast their shadows on each other and light is diminished. If the plane of the moon's orbit coincided exactly with Earth's, there would be an eclipse every month but I have offset the moon's orbit by a few degrees. Think of the many times you overshadowed the importance or reputation of someone, putting them into rejection's orbit!

NOVEMBER 29

My word has therapeutic value. All My words become alive through experience. I cleanse you from all unrighteousness as you confess and repent of your sins. I create a clean heart and renew your spirit. I give you My peace, strength, and My song to sing in the night watches. I meet all your needs and I give My angels charge over you (Psalm 91:11). There isn't anything more therapeutic than My Word made alive in you!

NOVEMBER 30

How can you tell if a person is godly? Read Psalm 119. You can tell by a person's behaviour and their words whether they are following My precepts and delighting in My laws. They are people whose consciences do not condemn them. They will radiate an inner beauty that I have given and am perfecting. What is your countenance revealing to others? When My light is reflected in your eyes, others will take notice.

listen

DECEMBER

GOD IS CALLING

DECEMBER 1

Pride will keep many from the freedom of coming to Me. Deep within is a longing to know Me but they push that idea away from their conscious thinking and get busy with other things. I send others across their paths to remind them of My love but they close the door in My disciples' faces. Access to My love means putting off pride, and humbly acknowledging you are a sinner in need of a Saviour. Come.

DECEMBER 2

Many people build memorials for themselves and others. They remember the kindness or deeds of someone and decide to erect a memorial to keep their memory alive. So often these memorials are like dead wood, ready for the fire. The memory burns for awhile and then turns to ashes. My name, I AM, is a memorial to all generations. Each generation has opportunity to know Me!

DECEMBER 3

What are the things you still hold dear? Are they too precious to part with or are you able to give those treasures away? Can you not yet comprehend the depth of My love or the preciousness of it? The truth is that all your wealth and fame counts for nothing in the end, although they came to you by My hand. I promise to give you the treasures and hidden riches of secret places. Come.

DECEMBER 4

Many take My name in vain. I detest it. Many use My name to gain recognition for themselves. Many think they are in My Kingdom because they use My name to cast out devils. Many are deceived by the adversary. Read My Word again. What allows entrance to heaven? Except you be born again of My Spirit you can not enter in (John 3:3). By faith, accept Me. Eternal life cannot be earned.

DECEMBER 5

People named one of my planets Mercury. It is one of the smallest and is the closest to the sun. It is difficult for you to observe it but based on photographs, scientists have concluded that Mercury's surface is scarred with ancient craters made by meteorites. Those closest to Me will be attacked by flying meteorites of the enemy but your shield of faith will deflect them. I am your rear guard. Fear not.

DECEMBER 6

What is the world without Me? People play games—both political and spiritual. This grieves Me. They do not see the foolishness attached to such games. Truth evades the person hooked on games. Do not be caught up in power struggles and games of manipulation because there are penalties to pay. How are the countries doing that deny My existence? How I desire to help them if only they would ask Me.

DECEMBER 7

You are placed in a strategic position in your community. Allow My light to shine. As a beacon of light from a lighthouse warns the sailors of rugged shores or shoals so My prophets warn people of approaching danger. Choose to be guided by My Word to be a lighthouse of freedom to those around you. The darkness is dispersed when My light exposes the wickedness. I will forgive.

DECEMBER 8

Many are pretending to have divine knowledge of Me. Beware. Do not be led astray by wrong knowledge. Beware of those who read your handwriting or perceive to know your past history and your future. New cults and religions with false doctrines are springing up. Be increasingly familiar with My Word so you can stand against twisted human doctrines. My truth leads to everlasting life.

DECEMBER 9

Many of you are powerless and ineffective because you are drawing other water than Mine. When you choose to abide in Me and obey, then power is released in you through My Spirit. As I cried for Jerusalem in days of old (Luke 19) so I cry for those separated from the flock of God. Open your ears and eyes, and see what you are doing to each other. You are brothers and sisters. Can I bless when you devour?

DECEMBER 10

Echoes are a repetition of sound waves from some surface. Pictures of shipwrecks, rocks, and fish in the depths of the sea are drawn from echo-sounding equipment. Your echo chamber is your conscience. How many times have you heard a Scripture verse learned years before echo again in your mind bringing to remembrance an important truth? Or does it convict you? Listen to those echoes.

DECEMBER 11

Who are your teachers? What are they imparting to you concerning knowledge? Are you learning from their example or experience? How teachable are you? Is your new-found knowledge in harmony with Mine? I am more than a teacher who instructs in ways of right living. Those who truly love Me are open to My knowledge. I teach to open the eyes of your heart so salvation is reached.

DECEMBER 12

A new year is approaching fast. Are you out of your comfort zone yet? I desire to increase your faith. Are you out and about encouraging others? If you want faith to grow, go for something more challenging where you have to rely on Me. Be convinced that I am capable of delivering; that is My nature. You are anointed to bring forth fruit so let Me unlock your spirit to deliver my message.

DECEMBER 13

I am your Prophet, Priest and King. My testimony is the spirit of prophecy. If you dwell in Me, you are capable of moving in the prophetic realm. My grace and your faith can move mountains (Matthew 17:20). I will take you places you have never been before in your faith. One step at a time you will progress and learn My ways. You have what it takes to touch Me.

DECEMBER 14

Have you ever seen Me striving? I am God in whom is rest so if your mind tells you to strive, tell it to stop now! When you recognize such things you rekindle the anointing in you, and your mind becomes the mind of Christ. Just as the sun, moon and Earth have to line up for an eclipse to occur, your mind and soul have to line up with what I am saying.

DECEMBER 15

Seek Me while I am still to be found (Isaiah 55:6) for the hour will soon come when hearts wax cold and tremble at the things to come. Those who remain faithful to Me will receive added strength to endure all tribulation. Reunite with Me to keep aware of things to come. Peace is available as well as My love. Keep your eyes on Me to complete the tasks ahead.

DECEMBER 16

It is I who sharpens your spirit and quickens it for service. I hear the prayers of My people. Refer to My Word and use it, and I will adhere to My word. Deep in intercession, you'll learn the depths of My love for humankind. You will know the joy I display as I answer prayer. Continue in praise as it allows My Presence to be in greater measure around you. Keys of prayer and thanksgiving open doors.

DECEMBER 17

As a sparkle of light reflects off new-fallen snow so will the sparkle of My love lift your soul to new heights. Freshness and newness wait to be birthed in your situation. Changing a seemingly difficult situation around you is still something I delight in. Exercise your faith and tell Me how excited you have become. I love working out with you and seeing your maturity. Rejoice in what I have prepared for you.

DECEMBER 18

I see dangers before they become dangers. I have often rescued people out of the hand of the evil one. It is I who command angels to encamp about you. It is I who lift you up into heavenly places to give you My perspective. Have no fear for I am watching you continually. Appropriate the gifts given to you for you have many, and much is required of you. Obedience blesses you but also others—big time!

DECEMBER 19

Don't neglect the work of intercession. I place the burdens upon you so that you will give them back to Me. Intercessors are needed. If you only knew how my heart aches when I see people turning to ESP, transcendental meditation and other 'new age' gods. They have no idea what transpires when they yield to other gods. Many are the lords of this life but there is only one true God and one Mediator, Jesus Christ. Am I your Lord?

DECEMBER 20

I will set your feet a-dancing. You will rejoice once again as I strengthen your heart and renew your faith. Remember not the trials and tribulations but look to Me for I will sustain you and deliver you out of them. I will give you new songs to sing. Receive them and sing them. Be not satisfied with spurts of anointing but rather desire to be released in anointings so rich that healings of all kinds will occur.

DECEMBER 21

Can you relate to the older generation, younger people, or single people? I minister friendship to all ages. I have called you to be 'family'. I have called into being relationships—sharpen each other. Discuss Me. Honour the elderly in your midst; I have given them much wisdom through experience that they can share.

DECEMBER 22

Have you experienced the unexpected in your life? Just as a drunken driver loses control on roads or steers sharply to avoid an animal he thinks is on the road so it is for those whose ways are not directed by My Spirit. In an instant you may find yourself against a rock – bewildered, angry, defensive, and too proud to admit it. Allow Me to take control of the 'unexpected' in your life. The unexpected can become blessings.

DECEMBER 23

I can see the road ahead of you. As a person retires from their occupation and takes up new adventures or hobbies, they may become sensitized to new sounds in the symphony of life, sounds that were formerly drowned out because they have been preoccupied with other voices. What preoccupies your mind the most? You need not wait until you are retired to hear from Me. Be still and know I am God (Psalm 46:10).

DECEMBER 24

What seems like a giant puzzle now will soon come together as a tapestry. Piece by piece you will see your life being woven. The dark threads have served their purpose and now new coloured threads will mingle, creating contrasting beauty. I am the Master Weaver. I know what is needed. In the end the tapestry will resemble a thing of beauty. All will see that you have spent time with the Weaver.

DECEMBER 25

Time is marching on. Tell others of My love for them. Tell them I was born in Bethlehem. I am the Living Word and have dwelled among them. Tell others they need to hear from Me. If they are open they will hear Me calling. Tell them that though theirs sins be as scarlet My blood washes them away and cleanses them (Isaiah 1:18). Tell them I make all things new. They become a new creation in Me (2 Corinthians 5:17). Tell them I love them.

DECEMBER 26

You have felt both repulsion and attraction towards Me. Like opposite poles of a magnet I either attract or repulse people. I have been drawing you tenderly into My sphere of influence like a magnet pulls magnetized objects to itself. My way can only be repulsive if your heart is leaning toward the things of this world. Know Me—it is not that difficult to come and give your Creator a chance. Eternity is at stake.

DECEMBER 27

Have you seen a road or home under construction? Surveying, grading, hammering, nailing, paving, roofing, tiling—the stages are numerous. Is there a reconstruction needed in your life? I have a divine construction license. I mould and form you without the nails, the lumber, the pavement. Stubbornness needs repair as it stands in the way of salvation values.

DECEMBER 28

I welcome back with outstretched arms all who have strayed and desire to come back to My fold. Your journey off the narrow path has brought many a tear and heartache but remember that I will rejoice over all prodigals coming home (Luke 15). Consider it a homecoming, a celebration, a day to remember. You were once lost and now are found. New avenues open as you return to Me.

DECEMBER 29

Never has there been a day like this day. Recall My kindnesses to you. Recall the works I have performed, the mercies I have shown. Recall the gift of salvation I have provided. Recall that My light has guided you. Recall My Word to you and all the gifts I have provided. Recall My promises and recall the Holy Spirit in the heart of the believer. Recall My communication with you and be thankful.

DECEMBER 30

Golden sunsets are pleasing to the eyes. How often have you desired to have them linger just a little longer so your eyes could behold the beauty? How precious are the golden sunset years of those who have committed their lives to Me. Their cry is for the lost and dying. I take pleasure in those who have endured and have been refined with My fire. I welcome those in their sunset years as they draw near.

DECEMBER 31

As the light of a new year breaks forth so shall My Spirit burst forth on those who love Me and desire My ways. Songs of laughter shall fill their hearts. A new wave of My Spirit is coming your way. Forget what happened last year and anticipate the best. Become a receiver of My grace as new waves of hope and love are showered down from above. Wells of refreshing are opened for the tasting. I love you.

prayer of
RECEIVING CHRIST

Dear Lord Jesus, I know I am a sinner, and I come to you now to receive you as my Saviour and Lord. Forgive all my sins as I recognize only You can forgive them. Come into my life and transform me. I invite you into my heart but also ask You to baptize me in the Holy Spirit. Help me to walk in the Spirit of love and truth, obedient to Your Word all the days of my life. Thank You for Your forgiveness and love.

AMEN

ABOUT THE AUTHOR

Helen Pasanen was born in Kirkland Lake, Ontario, Canada in 1942. She lived in Larder Lake, Ontario until 1950 when her parents, Hilda and Paavo Aspila, moved to Deep River, Ontario where she met and married Arthur A. Pasanen, a nuclear physicist working at Atomic Energy of Canada.

They have lived in Downsview, Mississauga and Erin, Ontario until they moved to Brantford, Ontario in 2016.

They have three children—Liisa, Paivi-Lee and Paul. All are married. Arthur and Helen have three grandchildren, three step-grandchildren and eight great-grandchildren.

At the age of fifty, Helen became an ordained minister, and holds credentials with Global Christian Ministry Forum in Canada.

Helen has joined her husband, Arthur, in the Gideon ministry, sharing the Gospel and distributing God's Word whenever possible. They have been married for 56 years.

JOURNEYS
to Unknown Spiritual Frontiers

Discovering God through
Obedience and Sharing

HELEN S. PASANEN
WITH ARTHUR A. PASANEN, M.S.E.

ALSO AVAILABLE:

JOURNEYS TO UNKNOWN SPIRITUAL FRONTIERS

ISBN: 978-1-4866-1653-4

What would you do if the Lord sent you a dream about a young woman, and then the next day, there she was—standing in front of you in the check-out line at your local gas station? Would you use this opportunity to witness, or would you shy away from following Holy Spirit because you don't feel adequately trained, or you fear rejection and embarrassment?

In *Journeys to Unknown Spiritual Frontiers*, Helen Pasanen and her husband, Art, focus on Spirit-led experiences in which they have seen the Glory of God manifested as part of the routine of daily life. You will discover examples of how a shy, introverted scientist has been able to share the hope in Jesus in a simple, loving way by sharing His faith story.

Included are Helen and Art Pasanen's testimonies of supernatural experiences as evidence of the Glory of God being manifested in our time, plus an account of Helen's call to prophetic intercession.